Davenport's Pennsylvania Wills And Estate Planning Legal Forms

DAVENPORT'S PENNSYLVANIA WILLS AND ESTATE PLANNING LEGAL FORMS

2024 EDITION

written by attorneys Alex Russell and Robert Maxwell

SEE BOOKS AND LEGAL FORMS AT WWW.DAVENPORTPUBLISHING.COM

COPYRIGHT © 2024 -- ALEX RUSSELL

CREATIVE COMMONS LICENSE. This work is also licensed under a Creative Commons Attribution-NonCommercial-NoDerivatives 4.0 International License.

GOVERNMENT WORKS. No claim is made to copyright or ownership of government materials.

SOME STANDARD FORMS. No copyright or ownership is claimed of "standard" forms or leading forms for the state which are provided in this book, but fair use and privilege to use is claimed. Makers of such forms (often a state agency or hospital) have agreed by word, act, and implication the forms may be used and copied if no profit is sought and no substantial changes made to them. Such makers if not a lawyer or law firm are barred from profit or advantage in practicing law by making forms then limiting use. Forms and other related materials are used here for educational purposes only. Authors strongly believe in a religious duty to help people and do charity.

PUBLICATION DATA
(informal, library may use different data)

Names: Russell, Alex, 1972- author; Maxwell, Robert, 1960- author

Title: Davenport's Pennsylvania Wills And Estate Planning Legal Forms 2024 Edition

Other Titles: Davenport's Wills

Description: Davenport Publishing 2024

Suggested Identifiers: 9798360698074, LCCN 2021909030, 9798748423373

Subjects: LCSH: Wills--United States;
Wills--United States--Forms;
Estate Planning--United States;
Legal Forms

Classification: LFF KF755 .C55 2024 (or as library chooses)
DDC 346.73 Rus--dc24 (or as library chooses)

9 8 7 6 5 4 3 2 1 0 0 0 0 0 2 4

PERMISSION TO COPY AND USE BOOKS FOR FREE

To help people and groups publisher and authors of the book allow mostly free use by giving all a "Creative Commons Attribution-NonCommercial-NoDerivatives 4.0 International License".

Basically as image below shows copying or use is OK if it still shows it's **by** the named authors, is **non-commercial** with no price charged, and has **no derivatives** which means no big changes.

Most users face no limit on copying, using, holding in library to loan out, or giving out copies.

Permission is given to change margins and formatting, do small changes, and cut any blank pages that may occur (but double-check page numbers and table of contents page numbers).

Printing on only 1 side of pages avoids complication of writing on back. Text margins are .75 inches. To do a book not a pamphlet increase left (inside) and decrease right (outside) margins.

Users can design a cover they like but the book title and author names must still appear on it.

Email questions to **davenportpress@gmail.com**.

(This work licensed under a Creative Commons Attribution-NonCommercial-NoDerivatives 4.0 International License.)

FOR FREE COPIES USE WWW.DAVENPORTPUBLISHING.COM OR BUY AT AMAZON.COM.

WARNING

THIS PUBLICATION IS NOT A SUBSTITUTE FOR LEGAL ADVICE. Publisher and authors say and warn this publication is not giving any legal, accounting, or other professional services or advice, which if wanted can be obtained by consulting in person an attorney or some other professional. **No attorney-client relationship or any relationship creating a duty or obligation is agreed to or created by the purchase or use of this publication or forms.**

BOOKS AND FORMS FOR OTHER STATES ARE AVAILABLE, SEE WWW.DAVENPORTPUBLISHING.COM FOR INFORMATION

CHAPTER	TABLE OF CONTENTS	PAGE NUMBER
CHAPTER 1 – BOOK BASICS, LIST OF FORMS, AND INFORMATION FORM		1
CHAPTER 2 – LEGAL TERMS AND PROPERTY LAW		5
CHAPTER 3 – WILL BASICS		7
CHAPTER 4 – WILL GIFTS INCLUDING RESIDUE CLAUSE		10
CHAPTER 5 – DEBT, MARRIAGE, AND YOUNG CHILD ISSUES		15
CHAPTER 6 – BASIC IDEAS ABOUT HEALTH CARE FORMS		18

WILL RELATED FORMS

CHAPTER 7 – FORM 1: LAST WILL AND TESTAMENT (STANDARD)		19
CHAPTER 8 – FORM 2: LAST WILL AND TESTAMENT (GUARDIAN)		23
CHAPTER 9 – FORM 3: SELF-PROVING AFFIDAVIT		27

HEALTH CARE FORMS

CHAPTER 10 – FORM 4: DURABLE HEALTH CARE POWER OF ATTORNEY AND HEALTH CARE TREATMENT INSTRUCTIONS (LIVING WILL)		29
CHAPTER 11 – FORM 5: DO NOT RESUSCITATE		39

GIVING POWER FORMS

CHAPTER 12 – FORM 6: GENERAL DURABLE POWER OF ATTORNEY		44
CHAPTER 13 – FORM 7: MEDICAL CONSENT AUTHORIZATION (OVER CHILD)		49
CHAPTER 14 – FORM 8: STATEMENT OF CONTRARY INTENT (OVER BODILY REMAINS)		52

APPENDIX: HOW TO GET FORMS AND SAMPLE FILLED OUT FORMS		54

CHAPTER 1
BOOK BASICS, LIST OF FORMS, AND INFORMATION FORM

ESTATE PLANNING IS MOSTLY DOING SIMPLE THINGS IN 3 AREAS

This book helps Pennsylvania people do Estate Planning documents to control property, money, children, health care, funeral, and more if later absent, sick, or dead. This book has 8 legal forms for Pennsylvania.

WILL RELATED FORMS

Form 1. Will (Standard) – a Will (also called a "Last Will And Testament") lets a person control things after their death like who gets money and property, who is Executor, and if easier legal options can be used.

Form 2. Will (Guardian) – Will with part added to name a person to be Guardian to care for a minor child under 18 if needed (like if both parents later die) and also manage a minor child's property and money.

Form 3. Self-Proving Affidavit – optional form done with a Will to later help show it was signed right.

HEALTH CARE FORMS

Form 4. Durable Health Care Power Of Attorney And Health Care Treatment Instructions (Living Will) – lets a person name someone to if needed control health care (this is the "Power of Attorney" part), and also say what health care to stop if later doctors think more care won't help (this is the "Living Will" part).

Form 5. Do Not Resuscitate – these are really 2 forms to do serious act of <u>immediately</u> refusing medical care, and these are short so paramedics can read them fast so they can be used outside any care facility.

GIVING POWER FORMS

Form 6. General Durable Power Of Attorney – lets power over money, property, and more be shared during life with someone like a spouse or friend so they can do things to help.

Form 7. Medical Consent Authorization (Over Child) – lets a parent share power over medical care of a child under age 18 with someone so they can watch a child and make medical decisions if suddenly needed.

Form 8. Statement Of Contrary Intent (Over Bodily Remains) – lets a person be named to control funeral and related matters, and this is done only if a person doesn't want closest family to do this.

BOOK IS SHORT, HAS FORMS, USES EMPHASIS, AND SUITS MOST PEOPLE

This book is short and may read rough but can be read fast. Long books often lead to misunderstanding and skimming. This book has many legal forms to see but <u>most people use just a few of these legal forms</u>. For emphasis paragraph titles, underlining, and boxes are used. This book capitalizes some legal words like Will, Testator, and Agent but this is optional. To save room some small words are skipped and end quote marks put before punctuation. This book covers the main U.S. legal ideas on Estate Planning and major ways state law is different. This book can't cover all issues but should suit people without any strange situations or wishes. <u>Strange situations or wishes that may need research or a lawyer include</u>: a) strange gift plans for property and money, b) wealth over $5 million, c) big medical concerns like extreme age, d) property or money going to a person with a disability or special needs, and e) wish to move or hide assets to qualify for government help.

LEGAL FORMS CAN HELP MANY AND THIS BOOK HAS STANDARD FORMS

Legal forms are good at most things involved in Estate Planning and can make binding legal documents. Instead of legal forms a lawyer can be used for Estate Planning but this can be costly, take months, and they can make mistakes. In life people often pick a cheaper option. Note, often a hospital, charity, state agency, or state legislature has made a form most people use and call the "standard form", and doctors, judges, and other people may not like to follow different things. Most people use only a few legal forms in this book.

LEGAL DOCUMENTS MAY NEED TO BE WITNESSED OR NOTARIZED

To be legal certain legal documents need to be "witnessed", which is someone watching a form be signed. Some documents need to be "notarized" where a person who is a "notary" sees it signed and then notarizes it. A notary (also called a "notary public") can be found using the phonebook and are at some banks, brokers, courts, law offices, libraries, and mail-copy centers. The words "subscribe" and "execute" means a person signed a document, and "acknowledgment" means a person said they signed it. If a person signs a document in a foreign language it is usually binding. The term "respectively" in a form means "in the order just stated". When filling out a legal form except for signatures the other parts can be filled in by a person not signing the form, and using pencil is fine except for signatures. Once done often people try to keep the original document and hand out copies. People can have everyone sign many copies to have many copies with ink signatures. A "person doing a legal document" and "doing a form" means the form is for and mainly affects that person.

BY LAW A PERSON CAN CONTROL THESE ISSUES BUT IT'S OFTEN NOT VITAL

Estate Planning is usually easy to do since by law a person mostly has full power to control these things. Given this usually judges, doctors, and other people mostly just ask: "Based on what a person wrote what did they likely want done?" It is also easy because simple documents can mostly do these things and simple words can be written in to do things. In reality Estate Planning is often not worth spending a lot of resources doing since it often doesn't greatly change the costs, taxes, delays, and later work in these areas. This is especially true for young people under 40. Many people spend more resources on getting life insurance.

SOME LESS COMMON OR LESS USEFUL FORMS ARE NOT IN THIS BOOK

- A "Codicil" can modify a Will but it is easier and legally safer to just rewrite the whole Will.
- Some people do a "Pet Trust" to help a pet, but it's easier to just give money in a Will to who gets the pet.
- Some people do a "Revocable Living Trust" so a Trust with a Trustee holds property or money during their life or later, mostly done to avoid small delays, costs, and work after death (by "avoiding probate"). But this is rare as it can require much work to move a person's property and money to a Trust and cause years of hassle.
- "Childrens Trust" papers can be done so upon a death a Trust gets things for a minor child to manage till 18, but this is uncommon due to possible costs and hassles and since it rarely matters (as this book explains).
- Organ donation forms are not included since usually this is done in papers for a drivers license or state ID.
- As this book explains later, a gift list or memo to add small gifts to a Will is rarely used in Pennsylvania.

INFORMATION FORM CAN HELP TELL FAMILY AND FRIENDS THINGS

People can do some kind of "Information Form" that many banks, lawyers, and planners suggest so any family or friends after a death will know helpful things about assets, debts, documents, and personal wishes. People can staple financial records and other pages to it. See form on the next pages to use if wanted.

INFORMATION FORM FOR ESTATE PLANNING

For more space attach copies of form or blank pages. Keep pages by Will or other place for Executor or family.

1. Personal Information (Name, Birthdate, Social Security number, special family details, other)**:**

2. Real estate, vehicles, and other major tangible property (especially if people may not find them):

3. Non-tangible assets like stocks, accounts, investments, loans owed you, and business interests:

4. Possible income or insurance like pensions, retirement, disability, insurance, or contracts:

5. Debts owed by you like credit card, loan, student loan, mortgage, car loans, and accounts payable:

6. Names and information of professionals used (attorneys, accountants, brokers, doctors, others):

7. Computer passwords and helpful files, document places, and safes or safe-deposit boxes code/key:

8. Other helpful things, wishes for funeral, special requests, and last messages to family and friends:

CHAPTER 2
LEGAL TERMS AND PROPERTY LAW

THERE ARE BASIC TERMS AND IDEAS IN ESTATE PLANNING

Some legal terms and ideas are basic to Estate Planning.

■ "Estate Planning" is about people doing legal documents to control things if later absent, sick, or dead. After a document is done people are still mostly free to transfer property, instruct doctors, or change forms.

■ "Probate" is a legal process to do things after someone's death like transfer property, handle creditors, and authorize a Guardian. Due to changes in the law probate is now often informal, faster, and less costly.

■ A "Will" or "will" (this book uses upper case "W") is a legal document done to control issues after death. The phrase "Last Will And Testament" is used since a Testament use to be a separate page done with a Will.

■ An "Executor" is a person named in a Will to do things after someone's death. If no Will names someone a judge names an "Administrator" to do this. "Personal Representative" is a blanket term for both these 2.

■ A person doing a Will is called the "Testator" or "Will maker". Before about 1995 a woman Testator was often called a "Testatrix" and woman Executor called an "Executrix" but this is no longer often said or written.

■ If no valid Will is done a person is "intestate" and then a dead person's property and money is transferred to a spouse, children, and family as intestate law says. Some people a fine with this. This is covered later.

■ A person who died is called the "decedent" or "deceased". A person getting a Will gift is usually called a "recipient", "beneficiary", or "heir" if related (they "inherit"). "Survive" or "surviving" is to be alive after someone else died. The term "descendants" or "issue" usually means a person's children and grandchildren.

■ Legally property is: 1) "real property" which is land and buildings ("real estate"), 2) "fixtures" which are things tied to real property (like fences, cables, carpets, and wired-in appliances), or 3) "personal property" which is all else (like household items, clothes, tools, cars, jewelry, art, moneys, accounts, and stocks),

■ A person under age 18 is usually called a "minor" and often a parent or guardian helps them do things. A minor or other person not reasonably able to make wise decisions lacks "capacity" and is "incapacitated".

■ A document giving power to someone is often called a "Power of Attorney" where the "Principal" gives power to someone called the "Agent" or "Attorney-in-Fact" (but they need not be an actual attorney).

■ Pennsylvania state law is called the "Pennsylvania Statutes" or sometimes the "Consolidated Statutes". Each law is usually called a statute which is shown by a "§" symbol. A reference to a law may look like, for example, "12 Pa. Statutes § 192". Wills are handled by the "Orphan's Court" in the "Register of Wills" office.

■ The "estate" or "probate estate" means all property and money of a dead person that at death or soon after didn't automatically legally go to new owners. Importantly, the estate is also the name for a temporary entity run by an Executor to do things after a death (it's like a small corporation that lasts a year or so).

PERSON CAN ONLY GIFT IN WILL WHAT THEY OWN AT DEATH

A person can only gift by Will things they own, so people should think about or research what they own. Basically by law a person usually owns all they earn as wages and salary, owns their share of income and profit tied to property they own, and owns or partly owns any things their money buys or improves. For items with "title" documents (real estate or vehicles) or where there is a "listed owner" (like accounts) the named persons are owners unless there are special circumstances. But a person during life is still free to do things, so people should try to notice if they sell or give away property they also name in a Will gift.

THINGS OWNED IN SPECIAL WAYS MAY LIMIT GIFTING IN A WILL

A person should consider if they own real estate or other property in special ownership ways which may limit gifting by Will. Laws vary in different states but some common special ways of ownership are:

- "joint tenant with right of survivorship" or similar legal options might be used in papers, so at a death property goes automatically to other named owners despite what a Will says (this is often how spouses hold a home);
- papers say a "life estate" exists, so then if a life of someone ends the other people in papers get item; and
- "Trust property" occurs if paperwork made a Trust entity and then property was transferred into it or this is set to occur, so then the Trust papers control where things put in the Trust go after someone's death.

Simple "joint ownership" with many owners can occur if people do joint papers, all agree to it, buy with joint funds, or if a gift was to many people. Wills can gift joint property, like "I give my half of boat to Ed Hu".

NON-PROBATE TRANSFERS THAT HAPPEN AUTOMATICALLY IGNORE A WILL

Importantly, some money or property of a decedent may automatically transfer on death or soon after to new owners if certain arrangements were made earlier. This is called "non-probate property". Such things transfer as arranged even if a Will names the same items. Examples are: a) a "designated beneficiary" form was done to name people to get an investment or account, b) transfer-on-death accounts were used, and c) real property is held by 2 people as "joint tenants with survivorship" or similar so at a death the surviving person gets things. Life insurance usually goes to the named beneficiary. Also, usually property in a Trust will ignore a Will and transfer as papers say. Trying to do non-probate transfers for all things is called "avoiding probate", but this is rarely done since it can be a hassle, has small benefits, and may fail. People should consider non-probate transfers that will occur automatically at a death and consider what will be left.

USUALLY NO FEDERAL OR STATE TAX IS OWED DUE TO A DEATH

Unless a person is rich rarely is tax owed at a death. A "Federal Estate And Gift Tax" exists but it only starts when a tax credit is used up that covers $13.61 million in 2024 or later. Pennsylvania has an "Inheritance Tax" but most people won't owe much for this. By law a spouse and children under 21 of the decedent don't owe this tax (adopted and step children too). Most other relatives pay a low 4.5% rate (like a child over 21, grandchild, and a parent). Brothers or sisters pay 12%. Other people pay 15%. For example, if a decedent left $600,000 of property or money and half goes to a spouse, and $100,000 goes to a child, and a sister, and a friend, then the spouse and kids owe zero tax, the sister owes 12% or $12,000, and the friend owes 15% or $15,000 (so just $27,000 of tax is owed on $600,000).

CHAPTER 3
WILL BASICS

A WILL LETS A PERSON CONTROL THINGS AFTER THEIR DEATH

A Will is a legal document done by a person to control some things after their death. A person doing a Will is called the "Testator" or "Will maker". In Pennsylvania a Testator <u>when signing</u> must be at least age 18, of sound mind (rational with sufficient memory), and not be under duress (unfair pressure or threat).

KEEP SIGNED WILL IN SAFE PLACE IT CAN BE FOUND AFTER A DEATH

A Will should be kept so it can be found within days of a death, like in a desk, drawer, safe, with a person, or less often a safe deposit box. It may help to tell family how to get a Will. In the distant past many people while alive filed their Will at the local courthouse for safekeeping but this is almost never done now.

OFTEN AT START OF A WILL A PERSON NAMES ANY SPOUSE AND CHILDREN

Many Wills <u>start with a place for a Testator to name any current living spouse and children of any age</u>. Natural or adopted children should be written here including any born outside marriage. People without this family can skip it or write "none". Not doing this may invalidate a Will by indicating a person lacks sufficient mental ability, or let a spouse or child not listed ask a judge to give them a share or all of the estate by claiming a Testator just forgot them. After listing family in a Will a Testator is often free to give them nothing.

IN PENNSYLVANIA USING WITNESSES FOR A WILL IS OPTIONAL BUT COMMON

Unlike many states in Pennsylvania <u>a Will just needs to be signed by a person doing the Will to be valid and having witnesses is not required</u>. However to use an unwitnessed Will after a death 2 people may have to sign papers or testify that people recognize the signature on the Will. Without witnesses a Will is a bit less likely to be later followed. Because of this doing a Will in Pennsylvania with witnesses is recommended.

PEOPLE IN A HURRY OR FIXING A THING OFTEN DO WILL WITH NO WITNESSES

Doing a Will with 2 witnesses is recommended. But in Pennsylvania it is somewhat common for people in a hurry, who want to fix a mistake in a Will, who just moved to the state, or who are about to go on a trip to quickly do a Will without having 2 persons as witnesses. Young people are especially likely to do this.

TESTATOR AND WITNESSES CAN DO SELF-PROVING AFFIDAVIT WITH NOTARY

To avoid the need for any testimony or other proof to use a Will later many people also do a document called a "Self-Proving Affidavit" which is signed using a notary. This is covered later in this book.

PROBABLY DO NEW DOCUMENTS IF DIVORCE, MARRY, HAVE CHILD, OR MOVE

Divorcing, marrying, having a new child, or moving to a new state can have big legal effects, and if any of these events occur it is recommended people do a new Will and other Estate Planning papers soon. To help a bit most states say a Will from another state is still valid if people move but this may be uncertain.

A WILL USUALLY IS SIGNED WITH 2 WITNESSES

A WILL USUALLY SHOWS IT IS A WILL AND IS SIGNED WITH 2 WITNESSES

In general usually a Will <u>must show it is a Will by its words</u>. Usually the person doing a Will then <u>signs at the end in front of 2 persons</u> acting as witnesses who then sign too. A Will just spoken on a video or audio recording usually has no legal effect. <u>Some people modify a Will to have 3 or 4 witnesses just in case this helps with things later</u>.

WITNESSES SHOULD BE AT LEAST 18 AND OFTEN NOT GETTING WILL GIFTS

A person to witness a Will must be at least age 18. It is best but not legally required a witness also not be very old, live far away, or be named in a Will to be Executor, Guardian, or similar. Note, in Pennsylvania unlike some states a Will is still valid if a witness is getting Will gifts. But many people just to <u>avoid the appearance of impropriety</u> pick witnesses who are "disinterested" which means they or their spouse are not named to get things in a Will. Often people used as witnesses are friends, neighbors, strangers, or family.

TESTATOR AND 2 WITNESSES SIGN THE WILL WHEN TOGETHER IN 1 ROOM

A person doing a Will usually signs it with at least 2 witnesses who also sign while all are in 1 room and see others sign. People showing others an ID is not required but is common. A Testator need not initial the Will pages. A Testator or witness usually <u>use their full legal name</u> unless they dislike and rarely use it. Witnesses only read the 1 paragraph they sign. Some Wills have each witness print their name and address. Legally <u>a Testator needn't say anything</u> but often they say a thing like, "My name is ____ this is my Will that I do voluntarily and ask you 2 people to witness". Lawyers call a person saying aloud a document is their Will as "publishing a Will". Some Testators chat about a Will with witnesses to help show they are of sound mind.

CANCELING OLD WILLS IS USUALLY NOT A PROBLEM

So a new Will is followed old Wills should be canceled ("revoked") but this is easy and rarely a problem. A new Will usually quickly says old Wills are revoked to cancel them, and all this book's Will forms say this. Or people can revoke an old Will by writing "void" or "cancelled" or "X" on it, preferably with a witness to this. Usually crossing out just part of a Will has no effect. Revoking a Will usually doesn't bring back an earlier Will.

MOST WILLS SAY PEOPLE MAY LATER DO INFORMAL PROBATE

Most Wills say after a death the family and friends may do "informal probate" which can avoid costs and delays. Informal probate often is done with just 1 court hearing and often is completed in well under 1 year.

MOST WILLS SAY TO SKIP COSTLY BOND FOR EXECUTOR AND OTHERS

Most Wills helpfully say no "bond" or "surety" is required for any Executor, Guardian, or similar person. A bond is insurance from a company to insure against misconduct. A Testator usually doesn't want a bond since the persons Testator names are trusted and them later needing a bond will cost the estate money.

MOST WILLS HAVE A MISCELLANEOUS PART WITH HELPFUL LANGUAGE

Most Wills have a "Miscellaneous" page with paragraphs of legal language to avoid some legal problems. This can help if later legal problems occur. A person doing a Will need not understand these paragraphs.

A WILL NAMES AN EXECUTOR TO DO THINGS AFTER DEATH

A WILL NAMES SOMEONE TO BE EXECUTOR TO DO THINGS AFTER A DEATH

Usually a Will names someone as "Executor" to act after a death. The law gives Executors many helpful legal powers, like to handle debts, find and collect and give new owners property and money, and do probate If a Will fails to name an Executor a judge can pick someone, but family may argue about who to suggest. Will gifts can go to a person named to be Executor. Often named Executor is a person's spouse, an adult child, a distant relative, a friend, or a local bank who agrees to it (this is rare since banks charge a high fee)

TERM OF PERSONAL REPRESENTATIVE IS NOW USED IN WILLS

As just said above, a person named in a Will to do things after someone's death is called an Executor. If no Will names someone to do this and a judge has to name someone they are called an "Administrator". The term of "Personal Representative" is used as a blanket term for both of these. In recent years most Pennsylvania Wills to avoid some legal issues use the term Personal Representative and not Executor.

EXECUTOR CAN BE PAID A SMALL AMOUNT BUT THIS IS OFTEN SKIPPED

Pennsylvania law says a person can ask to be paid for their hours of work as Executor. For example, an Executor who spent 4 hours of work a week for 50 weeks might ask to be paid a rate of $40 per hour, which means $8000 might be paid. Unlike some states Pennsylvania does not usually pay an Executor a percent of the property and money the decedent left. In actual practice most Executors later just skip asking for any pay so as to not owe income tax on pay and to leave more resources in the estate to carry out Will gifts.

PROPERTY AND MONEY OF DECEDENT PAYS ALL OF EXECUTOR'S EXPENSES

Expenses an Executor has like for insurance, utilities, repairs, funeral, mortgage, lawyer, and probate costs are usually by law paid for with money or property of the decedent who died. Any lawyer an Executor hires usually is paid an hourly rate or a fixed sum that the lawyer and Executor agree on.

EXECUTOR IS PERSON AT LEAST 18 AND SECOND PERSON RARELY NEEDED

A person to be Executor must be at least age 18 and usually not have a bad criminal record like a felony. A person not residing in Pennsylvania can be Executor but being local makes work easier. Naming 2 people to both be Executor is allowed but rare due to the risk of arguments and delays, and since any 1 person named should be trusted. People can name a 2nd person to be Executor if the 1st person is not later available but most skip this since this rarely occurs and if needed a judge can always just pick someone. To add such a 2nd person a person can write: "or if they're reasonably unable to serve I name ____ to serve".

CHAPTER 4
WILL GIFTS INCLUDING RESIDUE CLAUSE

MAIN USE OF A WILL IS TO WRITE GIFTS TO HAPPEN AFTER DEATH
Most people use a Will mainly to legally say what happens to their property and money after their death, usually by writing down various Will gifts to occur when they die. Verbal and even writings about this are not usually valid if not in a written Will. A Will can control property acquired after it was signed. The end of this chapter covers "intestate law" which says where a person's things go at death if no valid Will handles this.

RESIDUE CLAUSE IS CATCH-ALL THAT HELPFULLY GIFTS ANYTHING LEFT
Most Wills by their end have a Residue Clause to gift property or money not already gifted in a Will or used other ways, often called a "catch-all" or "left-over" clause. This is covered later in this chapter.

GIFTING IN A WILL USING SIMPLE WORDS OFTEN IS BEST
Making gifts in a Will using simple words is often best, using words like "I give to" and "I gift to". This is legally fine and avoids confusing legal words like "bequest", "devise", and "legacy" which few people know.

A PERSON IS MOSTLY FREE TO GIFT THEIR THINGS AS WANTED
A person is mostly free to give at death their money and property as they want. But creditors a decedent owed money, a spouse, and minor children under age 18 may have some rights which this book later covers.

WILL CAN DO SPECIFIC GIFTS TO GIFT PARTICULAR PROPERTY
Most Wills have "specific gifts" to gift <u>particular things</u>. Specific gifts can be any property, like "I give boat to Ed Blom" and "I give UBank account #84553873 to Sue Wu". If a gift is not clear the law assumes all of a kind of thing is given, like "I give jewelry to Ann Po" means <u>all</u> jewelry. But gifting specific property can have surprises like value of items can change, or a Will gift may later fail to occur if property is not owned at death.

WILL CAN DO GENERAL GIFTS LIKE OF MONEY
Wills can do "general gifts" where what is gifted is not particular property but can be flexibly chosen, like "I give 1 of my 3 cars to Ed Po" which lets an Executor pick which car. The usual general gift is money, like "I give $5 to Ed Hu". Money gifts are easy to write, let equal gifts be made, and are legally safer for many reasons. To carry out money gifts an Executor usually uses accounts or sells some property in the estate.

CONDITIONS ON WILL GIFTS ARE RARE DUE TO POSSIBLE PROBLEMS
Putting conditions on a gift, like "I give Ann Poe $90 if she graduates college", can cause problems like years of delay, risk of lawsuits, and big attorney's fees. Due to this any conditions on Will gifts are rare.

PROPERTY OR MONEY IN A JOINT GIFT GOES TO MULTIPLE PEOPLE
The same property or money in a "joint gift" can go to many people to each get a part. For example, "I give boat and all hats to Ann Baxter and Mary Ann Swanson" means each person owns part of every item. People later can split things by agreement or an Executor can decide how to divide items. If a person in a joint gift has died their part usually is left to transfer under a Residue Clause.

PERSON IN WILL GIFT USUALLY MUST SURVIVE OR GIFT DOES NOT OCCUR

Many Wills like this book's Will forms say a person named in a Will gift must survive (live past) the Testator for the gift to occur unless gift language specifically says different. If survival is not required for a Will gift what happens if a named recipient is dead can be unclear (state laws can be very complex). People doing a Will should consider how Will gifts to people dying before Testator usually have no effect. People if they see a person in a Will gift has died can re-do a Will or just let the Residue Clause handle it.

PEOPLE CAN ADD AN ALTERNATE BENEFICIARY LIKE FOR SPECIAL ITEMS

A person named in a Will gift dying before a Testator is rare, and if seen people can re-do a Will or let a Will's Residue Clause handle it. But some people to prepare for this chance maybe for special items write down an "alternate beneficiary", like "I give boat to Ed Liu but if they don't survive me to Ann Liu".

CAN SAY IF PERSON IN GIFT DIES THEN IT GOES TO LINEAL DESCENDANTS

A Will gift can say it goes to a person but if they don't survive then to their "lineal descendants per stirpes". Descendants are a person's children and grandchildren. "Per stirpes" means "by branch" and is about how to spread property and money, and it mostly tries to divide things so each family branch gets an equal share. Most Wills use "lineal descendants" language in a Residue Clause. An example shows how it works:

A Will may say: **"Clothes to Sue Wu but if they don't survive to their lineal descendants per stirpes"**, and this means if Sue Wu has died and her son Ken Wu is living and her other son Ben Wu has died but left 2 children then, legally, by law Ken Wu himself gets 50% and Ben Wu's 2 children each get 25%.

GIFT BENEFICIARIES CAN GET PERCENTAGE RATHER THAN EQUAL SHARE

If a Will gift goes to multiple people the law assumes equal shares, but if wanted percentages can be written in to make unequal gifts, like "I give boat 90% to John Smith and 10% to Mary Baker".

GIFTS IN WILL CAN GO TO A GROUP OR CLASS OF PEOPLE

To save work a Will gift can go to a group or class of people like certain family if who is meant is later easy to determine. People can say roughly how much in total is gifted to be clearer. Examples are: "I give $10 to each person on my 2018 soccer team" and "I give $10 to each of my grandkids so this is about $150 in total."

AFTER A DEATH FAMILIES OFTEN LET PEOPLE TAKE ITEMS UNOFFICIALLY

Many families unofficially let people take items in ways a dead person said, showed by stickers, or wrote on a note, which is often fine. If anyone objects a judge often has the Will and law be followed fully but later people can voluntarily retransfer items to do what the deceased person wanted.

UNLIKE MANY STATES IN PENNSYLVANIA GIFTS LISTS ARE RARELY USED

Many states let a person write out a short gift list (also called a memorandum) to add to an earlier Will more gifts they want to occur after death. This usually can only cover tangible personal property, like clothing, vehicles, household items, and jewelry. But Pennsylvania law makes it so easy to do or re-do a Will that most people find using gift lists is not worth the hassle and they just re-do a Will if they want to add more gifts. State law does not specifically authorize gifts lists or memorandums so most lawyers don't recommend them.

RESIDUE CLAUSE GIFTING ALL LEFT IS MAIN WAY USED TO GIFT THINGS

THE RESIDUE CLAUSE IS CATCH-ALL THAT HELPS GIFT ANYTHING LEFT

Most Wills by their end have a Residue Clause to gift any property or money not gifted earlier in a Will or used in other ways. Things transferred this way is called the "Residue". Many people gift most their money and property this way by intentionally not mentioning in a Will most things so the Residue Clause handles it. This avoids need to describe things and has less legal risk. After applying a Residue Clause if anything is somehow left then by law a decedent's closest heirs-at-law get things (this is their closest family).

USUAL RESIDUE CLAUSE HAS 2 PARTS

A short 2 part Residue Clause is usual and is used in this book's Will forms, and it has:

1) 1st space to name 1 or more persons to get things if they survive Testator (many name a spouse or closest family here), and if several people are named but only some survive then survivors split things, and

2) 2nd space to name persons to get things if all in the 1st space don't survive (many people name next close family or friends in this space), and if a person in 2nd space has died their descendants get their share.

EXAMPLE OF 2 PART RESIDUE CLAUSE:

"RESIDUE CLAUSE: I give money and property not gifted earlier, the residue:

  a) to ___John Paul Doe my husband___ who survive me with persons just named who survive me taking the share of non-survivors, then if anything remains

  b) to ___Sam Doe, Beth Wu, and Greta Fisher___ and if any of those just named do not survive me their part goes to their lineal descendants per stirpes."

In this example if John Paul Doe has survived he gets all things, but if John Paul Doe hasn't survived and also Sam Doe hasn't survived and he left 2 daughters then those 2 daughters split the 1/3 share of his (so get 1/6 each) and the other 2 persons in the second part Beth Wu and Greta Fisher get 1/3 each.

A FEW PEOPLE REWRITE RESIDUE CLAUSE TO HAVE 1 PART

A normal Residue Clause of 2 parts is often fine for most people. But a few people modify a Will to have a "1 Part Residue Clause" since it tends to gift to a group more equally and be simpler to understand. People with no spouse and no young children are likelier to do this change, but even they often don't bother. See Example below for exact words to use if people want to change to a 1 Part Residue Clause.

EXAMPLE OF 1 PART RESIDUE CLAUSE:

"RESIDUE CLAUSE: The rest, residue, and remainder of my estate, property of any kind and nature, and anything I have an interest in, I give to ___Adam Doe and Beth Wu___ who survive me and to lineal descendants per stirpes of any person just named who did not survive me."

In this example if Adam hasn't survived but had 2 children they each get 25%, and if Beth Wu survived she gets 50%. Or if Beth Wu also hadn't survived and had 5 kids they split her part and each gets 10%.

MUST SUFFICIENTLY DESCRIBE NAMES AND PROPERTY IN A WILL

PUTTING NAMES OF PEOPLE OR GROUPS IN A WILL IS FAIRLY EASY

Putting names in Wills is fairly easy. A judge or Executor assume a person in a Will meant people they know, so common names are OK unless 2 friends or family have the same name. Details can help if names won't be recognized or to be friendly, like "I give $5 to my nurse Sue Ax" and "I give $5 to loyal pal Ed Lee". If people used a nickname "also known as" or "a/k/a" may help, like "I give $5 to Dan Smith a/k/a Old Fishy". Gifts can go to a charity, government, or group, like "I give $10 to YMCA of USA", "I give $5 to Bucks County Library, Philadelphia", and "I give $50 to Wix Church, Houston, TX". People can phone for a charity's name.

PUTTING DESCRIPTIONS OF ITEMS IN WILL GIFTS IS FAIRLY EASY

Describing items in gifts is easy since people rarely own similar items. Often fine are gifts like: "I give ax to Ed Wu" and "I give big table to Ann Fox". It's OK to gift by category or list, like: "I give tools to Sam Lee" and "I give cow, van, and harp to Sue Hill". Financial assets can use plain words, like "bank accounts" or "stocks", but details can help, like: "US Bank account ending #1511". Gifting using a location is riskier as judges will ignore Will gifts if it seems items were placed to affect gifting and no "independently significant" life reason. So, "I give Ed Po items in safe and desk" judges might not follow, but "I give Ed Po hats in attic" likely is OK.

DESCRIBING REAL PROPERTY IS HARD IF NOT USING RESIDUE OR TITLE

The easier, legally safer way to transfer real property (real estate) at death is: 1) do nothing specific so it's handled by a Will Residue Clause, or 2) have a lawyer or agent put names in a deed or similar document so then named persons legally get things at someone's death. Most use these 2 ways to transfer real property.

Gifting real property other ways is harder though possible. Helpfully a Will gift of real property described by location legally does gift all land, buildings, and fixtures located there with no need to describe what's there.

It is possible to gift real property at a particular address with very plain words, like a house, fixtures, and land can be fully given by something like: "I give 81 Maxwell Street, Altoona, Pennsylvania, to Mary Ann Brown".

People can do a blanket gift giving all of a kind of property, like, "I give all real property and fixtures in Berks County, Pennsylvania to Ann Ivy Hill " or "I give all furniture and all bank accounts to Eric Paul Carlson".

Giving real property in a Will using a "legal description" is how many lawyers do it, but this can be hard to do. If using a legal description people must copy without mistakes the full legal description of maybe many lines into a Will with no abbreviation at all. A legal description might be found on a deed or on mortgage papers. Legal descriptions may refer to a "lot" or "blocks" on a map which is recorded in land records of a county, or it may refer to a path around the land borders with various angles, distances, and iron stakes.

CAN LEAVE SOME WILL GIFT LINES BLANK OR WRITE TO SAY SKIP

A person writing a Will can choose to not use some gifts lines in a Will legal form, like by just leaving them blank, writing things like "SKIPPED" or "NONE" in them, or using a computer to delete some gift lines. Judges and others usually do not care about neatness or empty spaces in Wills.

MOST STATES AND WILLS SAY PEOPLE TO GET GIFTS MUST SURVIVE 5 DAYS

Helpful laws in most states and all this book's Will forms say if a person dies within 5 days (120 hours) or simultaneously with a Testator, then they are legally seen as dying before Testator. This skips the need to prove exact time of death (like if people die in 1 accident), and avoids a Will gift or right to something going to someone who then soon dies within days (so an item may have to go through multiple probate proceedings).

LATER DIVORCE OR MURDER CANCELS WILL GIFTS TO A PERSON

Pennsylvania law says a person divorcing or murdering a Testator usually cancels Will gifts to the person.

INTESTATE LAW CONTROLS THINGS NOT HANDLED BY A WILL OR SIMILAR

A state's "intestate" law says <u>if a person dies with no valid Will</u> or <u>if anything is left after Will and other transfers are done</u> then certain surviving (living) family get money and property. Many people like how intestate law transfers things and choose to skip a Will, but often doing a Will has some other small benefits. <u>Pennsylvania intestate law is found in state law at 20 Pa. Statutes § 2101 and the following later statutes</u>. Basically, usually intestate law says about half and sometimes all property and money goes to any surviving spouse (if any), then half or any remainder goes to decedent's children (or if dead their own child gets that share), then next closest family like any living parents or brothers and sisters, and then to the state. For intestate law a legally adopted child counts but not foster-child or step-child.

SIMPLE WILL WITH MOST GIFTING DONE BY RESIDUE CLAUSE OFTEN IS BEST

<u>Writing a simple Will without many gifts, much left blank, and mostly using a Residue Clause is often best</u>.

If there is <u>no spouse and no children</u> often a person does a few small gifts, and then names some family or friends in the Residue Clause to get everything remaining.

If there <u>is only a spouse</u> often a person does small gifts to friends and family, then uses the Residue Clause of the Will to gift all left to the spouse, and then names a few fallback persons in the Residue Clause.

<u>A parent with young children if married to the other parent</u> often does small gifts to friends and family, then in the Residue Clause gives mostly to a spouse, and then names children as fallbacks in the Residue Clause.

<u>A parent with young children if not married or close to the other parent</u> often does small gifts to friends and family, and then uses the Residue Clause to gift all remaining to the children.

CHAPTER 5
DEBT, MARRIAGE, AND YOUNG CHILD ISSUES

THIS CHAPTER COVERS CERTAIN ISSUES THAT SOME PEOPLE CAN SKIP
This chapter covers debt, marriage, and young child issues, and some people can skip parts of this.

DEBT ISSUES

PAYING DECEDENT'S DEBTS MAY USE UP RESOURCES AND REDUCE GIFTS
If a decedent had debts then creditors owed may ask a judge to be paid from decedent's money or property before Will gifts and certain transfers occur. How debts are paid is set by state law and a Will need not describe this. Funds to pay debts come from decedent's money and property so may affect (in order) the Will Residue, Will general gifts, Will specific gifts, and non-probate transfers. Probate, health care, taxes, and funeral costs by law have some priority to be paid first. People should consider how paying debts may use up money or property, leaving less to carry out Will gifts. A spouse and family usually are not liable to pay a decedent's debts unless they actually guaranteed or co-signed for a debt. But for many reasons if a decedent had under about $30,000 plus a house often creditors don't bother trying to collect what is owed. Note, helpfully if a decedent who died left under $50,000 of money and property of any kind then a spouse or other closest family can use a "Small Estate Affidavit", and this lets them get ownership of most things without having to do most probate steps and without giving notice to creditors.

HOMESTEAD LAWS OR PUTTING FAMILY ON TITLE CAN PROTECT HOME
"Homestead" laws in most states say decedent's creditors can't seek payment by foreclosing and selling decedent's house if decedent's spouse or children under 18 are there (unless equity is big like over $1 million). Also, laws in some states say a spouse or minor children get ownership of decedent's house (or use for life) if decedent owned it and despite a Will trying to gift it to other people. Due to these laws most people gift any spouse or minor children the family house by Will or by naming them on the land title. Pennsylvania is very unusual and has less family protection of the homestead. To offset this most people in Pennsylvania hold the title to house jointly with a spouse or other family as "tenancy by entireties" or "tenancy with survivorship" so the house automatically goes to other people on title and any creditors can't affect a house.

SECURED DEBTS LIKE MORTGAGE OR VEHICLE LIEN ARE NOT PAID OFF
Laws in most states say do not pay off secured debts on property of a decedent like a house mortgage or vehicle lien even if other debts are paid by Executor or in probate. This avoids using up estate resources on paying these usually big debts and leaves more estate resources to carry out Will gifts and other transfers. Due to this, all this book's Will forms say do not usually pay off any secured debts. But if a Testator with a mortgage or lien wants to they can 1) put in a Will an order to pay (like, "Executor pay off the house mortgage"), or 2) gift enough money to pay off a secured debt to the person getting the property. Most banks let the new owners after a death keep paying monthly any secured debt like a mortgage or lien.

MARRIAGE ISSUES

PENNSYLVANIA USES SEPARATE PROPERTY LAW FOR SPOUSES

Pennsylvania like most states uses the Separate Property Law system that says a married person <u>mostly owns their money and property separately</u> and not jointly with a spouse. Due to this a married person is usually free to sell during life or gift by Will most of their money or property and not have to involve a spouse. But joint ownership by 2 spouses and not separate ownership <u>can arise in other ways</u>, like by agreement, both spouses paying part of the purchase price, if a gift was to both spouses, or if paperwork calls it joint.

COMMUNITY PROPERTY LAW APPLIES IN OTHER STATES FOR SPOUSES

There are 9 states mostly in the Western U.S. that use the Community Property Law system for any spouses (Arizona, California, Louisiana, Idaho, Nevada, New Mexico, Texas, Washington, and Wisconsin). This says property or money is owned 50/50 by spouses as Community Property if it's from mental or physical work while married (like wages or salary) or if items are bought or improved with any other Community Property. People recently moving from these states may face legal issues.

JOINT WILL OR SIMILAR BOTH SPOUSES SIGN IS NOT RECOMMENDED

Some couples who worry a lot try to sign a "Joint Will" or a "Contract To Make A Will" done by a lawyer which says spouses give all to the other if they die first, then says last living spouse gives to all children equally, and usually says a spouse may not change this. This is banned in some states and is rarely used.

SPOUSE IF UNHAPPY WITH WILL CAN CHOOSE ONE-THIRD ELECTIVE SHARE

Most states using Separate Property law like Pennsylvania to be fair <u>give a spouse if unhappy with what a Will gifts them a right to choose (elect) an "Elective Share" of their spouse's property and money instead</u>. Some states say the Elective Share is a percentage that increases with duration of marriage, often reaching 50% at 15 years. <u>Pennsylvania law is simple and says the Elective Share is 1/3 of the dead spouse's property and money with some small modifications</u>. If an Elective Share is chosen then Will gifts to spouse are not done, but Will gifts to other people are carried out like normal unless the property and money is needed to satisfy the Elective Share to the spouse. <u>Because of this often a married person gifts by Will and other ways mostly to a spouse (like at least 50%) to avoid them being upset and using an Elective Share.</u>

YOUNG CHILD ISSUES

WILL CAN NAME A GUARDIAN OF THE PERSON TO CARE FOR YOUNG CHILD

If a parent dies with a child under age 18 then any other natural or adopted parent (but not a step-parent) almost always automatically gets control of the child's care (including health care, school, and home issues). This won't occur only if the other parent will be unavailable a long time or is proven unfit in court which is rare. But just in case it is later needed (like later both parents of a child die) a Will often names a healthy and willing relative or friend as "Guardian of the Person" to give this care for a young child.

WILL CAN NAME A GUARDIAN OF THE ESTATE TO MANAGE CHILD'S PROPERTY

Since a child until age 18 can't legally easily control property including money a Will often names a person to be "Guardian of the Estate" of a minor to have the job of managing a young child's property and money. Many states call this a "Conservator" or a "Guardian of Property". This person says each month how to use property and money on a child's needs (like on school, living, and health care) and then usually at age 18 any money and property left is handed to the child. Any person paying things for a child can ask to be paid back. Judges may hold a yearly hearing on spending. As a nice 2nd option to avoid work and costs most Wills say an Executor may name a person (including themselves) as "Custodian" to manage things using the new helpful Uniform Transfers To Minors Act.

MOST WILLS NAME 1 PERSON TO CARE FOR CHILD AND THEIR PROPERTY

Most parents and this book's Will forms name the same 1 person to care for a child and also manage a child's property and money. People can change a Will to name different people for the 2 positions, but this is rarely worth it since parents dying is rare, rarely do children get much property or money, a person smart enough to handle a child often can handle money, and naming different people can lead to arguments and even costly lawsuits between people. Will gifts can go to someone named to be a Guardian.

PERSON TO HELP A CHILD MUST BE AT LEAST 18

To be a Guardian of any kind for a minor in Pennsylvania a person must be at least age 18 but they needn't live here. Later a judge can block a person as Guardian if they seem unfit, which usually means they have a history of criminal felonies, abuse, or fraud. The choice made by the last living parent is usually followed. If no Will names a person for a position or they're unavailable a judge can pick someone, but family may argue about who to suggest. Naming 2 people to act at the same time in the same position is rare since 2 persons may argue and any 1 person named should be smart enough to act alone. In rare cases a married couple is named for the same position but there can be problems if they divorce or disagree. Importantly, some Wills add a 2nd person to serve if the 1st person named is later not available, like by adding: "or if they are later unable to serve I name _____ to serve"). But most people skip naming a fallback person since it is rarely needed, if a problem is seen a Will can be redone by a person, and a judge can just pick someone if needed.

NAMING PERSONS TO HELP CHILD RARELY MATTERS

A child under 18 having parents die is rare so parents shouldn't worry much about naming people to help. A good U.S. study looked at 72,240 people under age 18 and found only 2014 had lost 1 parent (so 2.78%) and only 97 had lost 2 parents (so a very small 0.13%). *Parent Mortality Census SIPP Paper #288.*

CHAPTER 6
BASIC IDEAS ABOUT HEALTH CARE FORMS

BASIC IDEAS HELP PEOPLE UNDERSTAND CONTROLLING HEALTH CARE

Some ideas help people understand health care forms.

■ By law people control their own health care by telling doctors and others what they want <u>unless they're "incapacitated"</u> by insufficient ability to a) <u>communicate</u> verbally or by notes, b) be <u>rational</u>, or c) be <u>conscious</u>. In actuality most people keep control of their own health care till death or till no big treatment options remain, but people may worry they may be incapacitated a long time so they want to do health care forms.

■ If an adult 18 or older becomes incapacitated <u>the adult's closest family like spouse or adult child can make emergency decisions</u> but they usually must then rush to a judge to get further power if no legal document gives them full power over health care.

■ In forms a <u>person can be named to have control of health care</u> if needed who is often called "Agent". Forms about control of health care if people are later incapacitated are often called "Advanced Directives".

■ In forms people can give <u>written health care instructions that doctors, family, and Agent must obey</u>.

■ Parents do have power over health care of <u>their children under age 18</u>.

■ Some <u>young married people</u> give a spouse power over health care in case they are ever incapacitated. Some <u>young adults</u> give this power to parents. Young people are less often ill so often skip doing things.

■ Pain relief like pain drugs and comfort care is usually given even if forms say to stop or limit other care.

■ <u>Most people only do a single long health care form</u> that has a spot to give someone power over health care and a spot for instructions (this is often called a "Health Care Power of Attorney" though names vary).

■ For the rare cases when saying to stop health care likely matters due to extreme illness or old age:

-- most people do nothing special and trust family or Agent for health care to decide on stopping care based on many factors like pain, cost, hassle, suffering and time of treatment, beliefs, and chances of recovery;

-- a few people do a serious document to say to stop most health care if <u>later</u> doctors decide a person is incapacitated, is in bad medical condition (irrevocable terminal condition or unlikely to regain consciousness), and more medical care won't help (this document to stop care is often called a "Living Will" but names vary);

-- a few people do a serious document to <u>starting immediately</u> block certain health care (and this often is called a "Do-Not-Resuscitate" if about resuscitation or called a "Physician's Order" if about many treatments).

CHAPTER 7
FORM 1: WILL (STANDARD)

FORM 1 IS A STANDARD WILL THAT IS FLEXIBLE BUT WITHOUT A GUARDIAN

Form 1 is a flexible Will that lets a person control many things after their death. This form has no part about a Guardian so is for someone with no child under age 18.

THIS FORM IS A WILL WITH SEVERAL PARTS

The form starts with lines for a person to put their name (a full legal name is best but not required) and place of main residence (most put a county but some put a city). The Will is still valid if people later move.

Paragraph 1, "List Of Spouse And Children", lets a person write the names of any living spouse and children they have, or if none maybe write "none". This helps show a Testator has enough mental ability and memory to do a Will. Not listing a living spouse or child here can let an omitted person ask a judge to give them a share or all of a Testator's property and money by claiming they were accidently forgotten.

Paragraph 2, "Gifts", has many spaces to make either specific gifts of particular property or general gifts like of money. People can delete, copy and paste to add more, or leave blank these gift lines.

Paragraph 3, "Residue", has a Residue Clause to say any property and money left after other Will parts and other transfers is to be distributed in the way a person wrote in the blank parts of this paragraph.

Paragraph 4, "Administration", names a person to be Executor to do things after a person's death (some people especially in other states use the term "Personal Representative" for this).

Paragraph 5, "Miscellaneous", has paragraphs of legal language to help avoid certain legal issues.

Last paragraph is for the person doing the Will as Testator and witnesses to sign and put information.

USUAL RESIDUE CLAUSE HAS 2 PLACES TO NAME PERSONS TO GET THINGS

In a Will "Residue Clause" anything left over after other Will parts is transferred as the clause directs. Many people use a Residue Clause to gift most their things. In this Will form's Residue Clause there is:

1) a 1st space to name 1 or more persons to get the Residue, and if any named here have died before the Will maker then other persons named here in this 1st space take the dead person's share, and

2) a 2nd space to name people to get things if all people named in the 1st space have died, and if any people named in the 2nd space have died their shares go to "lineal descendants" like their children.

People often put in the 1st space a spouse or closest family or friends, and in 2nd space next closest people.

TESTATOR AND 2 WITNESSES WHILE TOGETHER SIGN WILL

The Will after being filled out (except bits intentionally left blank) must by law be signed by the person doing the Will (they are called Testator). Though legally optional for a Pennsylvania Will usually there also are 2 persons acting as witnesses who watch the Will be signed and then also sign and put their address.

LAST WILL AND TESTAMENT

I, _____, of _____, Pennsylvania do revoke all prior Wills and testamentary documents and do make, publish, and declare this as my Will. I am of sound mind and under no duress or undue influence and acting voluntarily.

1. LIST OF SPOUSE AND CHILDREN. To help show I am mentally competent and have sufficient memory to make a Will I wish to list any living spouse and living children I now have. I currently have the following living spouse and living children:

_____
_____.

2. GIFTS. I give these gifts in this Will, but to get a gift in this section the recipient must survive me except as otherwise stated below.

I give _____ to _____.

I give _____ to _____.

I give _____ to _____.

I give _____ to _____.

I give _____ to _____.

I give _____ to _____.

I give _____ to _____.

I give _____ to _____.

I give _____ to _____.

I give _____ to _____.

3. RESIDUE. I give the rest and residue and remainder of my estate, my money and property of any kind and nature, and anything I have an interest in so long as it was not transferred by other Will provisions, as follows:

  a) to _____ who survive me with persons just named who survive me taking the share of non-survivors, then if anything remains

  b) to _____ and if any of those just named do not survive me their part goes to their lineal descendants per stirpes.

4. ADMINISTRATION. I name, nominate, and appoint _____
as Personal Representative including for me, my Will, and my estate.

5. MISCELLANEOUS. The following applies to this Will and generally.

In this Will no part left unfilled is a mistake including spaces in the residue clause.

The facts support and I want Pennsylvania state law to apply to this Will and my estate.

If context allows the terms Personal Representative and Executor and Administrator are interchangeable. If context allows the terms Guardian of the Estate and Conservator and Guardian of Property and Custodian are interchangeable. Any such person has all powers and rights of the others.

I order that my just debts, funeral and related expenses, and taxes be paid as soon after my death as practical but only those items my Executor chooses to pay.

Priority of Will gifts of the same type is based on the order they are written.

The words "give" and "gift" also means a devise, bequest, grant, legacy, or similar.

I am intentionally not providing by Will or other ways for some family, including I am not providing for some children of mine and also children of a deceased child of mine.

If a gift Will reasonably mentions survival then survival is an absolute condition and anti-lapse laws or similar provisions have no effect and without survival the gift lapses. Unless a Will gift specifies otherwise if a Will gift goes to multiple recipients if any do not survive me the part to them lapses and instead goes to other surviving recipients.

No earlier transfer reduces a Will gift unless I usually called it a loan or advancement.

In this Will any gender or gendered word includes all genders, and the singular includes the plural and vice versa, and "they" can mean a single person or many persons.

Unless a Will specifically says otherwise a secured debt including a mortgage or lien shall not be paid off including by a Personal Representative or in probate, and a recipient of a Will gift of property takes it subject to debts. Also, no recipient of property who may lose it or who pays to keep it may have my estate or others pay or do exoneration.

If at my death I somehow no longer own, possess, or otherwise control an item in a specific gift then the gift is extinguished, including I want full ademption to apply.

I request and authorize any informal, summary, and quick probate or similar action. Any Personal Representative may act independently with no supervision of any court, including independent administration, and with no inventory, appraisal, or other action.

Any Guardian of any type, Conservator, Custodian, or other person managing a minor's property or money may use or invade the principal and sell property without court action.

I give any Personal Representative the a) fullest authority, discretion, and powers allowed by state law in any jurisdiction they may act, b) power to lease, sell, mortgage, convey, or keep property including real property in a manner and time they find helpful or proper, and c) authority to settle or pay claims or debts in time and manner they choose.

Any Personal Representative may access, manage, delete, modify, transfer, and

otherwise control any digital accounts and assets I had any interest in or power over.

Any Personal Representative, Executor, Administrator, Guardian of any type like for a person or estate, Conservator, Custodian, or other fiduciary under this Will or otherwise shall qualify and serve without bond, surety, security, surety bond, or similar.

No Personal Representative or any professional entitled to fair compensation shall be paid a percentage or share of my estate, property, or money even if that is standard.

The residue includes lapsed or failed gifts, insurance paid to the estate, digital assets, inheritances owed me, and all I had power of appointment or testamentary disposition over.

If evidence does not show it likely a person survived me by 120 hours (5 days) then for this Will and my estate they shall be deemed in all ways as having died before me.

Any Personal Representative may anytime transfer money or property of a minor under age 18 to a Custodian to serve under the Pennsylvania Uniform Transfers to Minors Act or similar law anywhere, and may pick a person to be Custodian including themselves.

To the extent allowed by law any Personal Representative should follow any writings I have done disposing of tangible personal property in the manner the writings indicate.

If part of this Will is by law invalid or unenforceable other provisions remain in effect.

TESTATOR

IN WITNESS WHEREOF, I, the Testator, declare I have voluntarily signed this Will on the ____ day of _____, 20____.

_____
Testator signature

WITNESSES
(optional in Pennsylvania)

The foregoing instrument was signed by the Testator in our presence and declared by the Testator to be the Testator's Will, and we, the undersigned Witnesses, sign our names hereunto to act as witnesses at the request and in the presence of the Testator, and in the presence of each other on the ____ day of _____, 20____.

_____   _____
Signature of Witness #1   Address of Witness #1

_____   _____
Signature of Witness #2   Address of Witness #2

CHAPTER 8
FORM 2: WILL (GUARDIAN)

FORM 2 IS A WILL WITH GUARDIAN PART FOR PERSON WITH YOUNG CHILD

Form 2 is a Will with a Guardian part to be used by a person with a minor child under the age of 18. A person doing a Will is called a Testator.

FORM IS A WILL WITH SEVERAL PARTS INCLUDING A GUARDIAN PART

The form starts with lines for a person to put their name (a full legal name is best but not required) and place of main residence (most put a county but some put a city). The Will is still valid if people later move.

Paragraph 1, "List Of Spouse And Children", lets a person write the names of any living spouse and children they have, or if none maybe write "none". This helps show a Testator has enough mental ability and memory to do a Will. Not listing a living spouse or child here can let an omitted person ask a judge to give them a share or all of a Testator's property and money by claiming they were accidently forgotten.

Paragraph 2, "Gifts", has many spaces to make either specific gifts of particular property or general gifts like of money. People can delete, copy and paste to add more, or leave blank these gift lines.

Paragraph 3, "Residue", has a Residue Clause to say any property and money left after other Will parts and other transfers is to be distributed in the way a person wrote in the blank parts of this paragraph.

Paragraph 4, "Administration", names a person to be Executor to do things after a person's death (some people especially in other states use the term "Personal Representative" for this).

<u>**Paragraph 5, "Guardian",** names a person as Guardian of the Person to care for minor children under 18 if needed (like if both parents die) and Guardian of the Estate to manage property and money of a child</u>.

Paragraph 6, "Miscellaneous", has paragraphs of legal language to help avoid certain legal issues.

Last paragraph is for the person doing the Will as Testator and witnesses to sign and put information.

USUAL RESIDUE CLAUSE HAS 2 PLACES TO NAME PERSONS TO GET THINGS

In a Will "Residue Clause" anything left over after other Will parts is transferred as the clause directs. Many people use a Residue Clause to gift most their things. In this Will form's Residue Clause there is:

1) a 1st space to name 1 or more persons to get the Residue, and if any named here have died before the Will maker then other persons named here in this 1st space take the dead person's share, and

2) a 2nd space to name people to get things if all people named in the 1st space have died, and if any people named in the 2nd space have died their shares go to "lineal descendants" like their children.

People often put in the 1st space a spouse or closest family or friends, and in 2nd space next closest people.

TESTATOR AND 2 WITNESSES WHILE TOGETHER SIGN WILL

The Will after being filled out (except bits intentionally left blank) must by law be signed by the person doing the Will (they are called Testator). Though legally optional for a Pennsylvania Will usually there also are 2 persons acting as witnesses who watch the Will be signed and then also sign and put their address.

LAST WILL AND TESTAMENT

I, _____, of _____, Pennsylvania do revoke all prior Wills and testamentary documents and do make, publish, and declare this as my Will. I am of sound mind and under no duress or undue influence and acting voluntarily.

1. LIST OF SPOUSE AND CHILDREN. To help show I am mentally competent and have sufficient memory to make a Will I wish to list any living spouse and living children I now have. I currently have the following living spouse and living children:
_____
_____.

2. GIFTS. I give these gifts in this Will, but to get a gift in this section the recipient must survive me except as otherwise stated below.

I give _____ to _____.

I give _____ to _____.

I give _____ to _____.

I give _____ to _____.

I give _____ to _____.

I give _____ to _____.

I give _____ to _____.

I give _____ to _____.

3. RESIDUE. I give the rest and residue and remainder of my estate, my money and property of any kind and nature, and anything I have an interest in so long as it was not transferred by other Will provisions, as follows:

  a) to _____who survive me with persons just named who survive me taking the share of non-survivors, then if anything remains

  b) to _____ and if any of those just named do not survive me their part goes to their lineal descendants per stirpes.

4. ADMINISTRATION. I name, nominate, and appoint _____ as Personal Representative including for me, my Will, and my estate.

5. GUARDIAN. I name, nominate, and appoint _____
to be Guardian of the Person of any minor child of mine and also to have care, authority, custody, and other control of them. I name, nominate, and appoint this same person to be Guardian of the Estate for any minor child and to have care, control, and power over their property, money, and estate.

6. MISCELLANEOUS. The following applies to this Will and generally.
    In this Will no part left unfilled is a mistake including spaces in the residue clause.
    The facts support and I want Pennsylvania state law to apply to this Will and my estate.
    If context allows the terms Personal Representative and Executor and Administrator are interchangeable. If context allows the terms Guardian of the Estate and Conservator and Guardian of Property and Custodian are interchangeable. Any such person has all powers and rights of the others.
    I order that my just debts, funeral and related expenses, and taxes be paid as soon after my death as practical but only those items my Executor chooses to pay.
    Priority of Will gifts of the same type is based on the order they are written.
    The words "give" and "gift" also means a devise, bequest, grant, legacy, or similar.
    I am intentionally not providing by Will or other ways for some family, including I am not providing for some children of mine and also children of a deceased child of mine.
    If a gift Will reasonably mentions survival then survival is an absolute condition and anti-lapse laws or similar provisions have no effect and without survival the gift lapses. Unless a Will gift specifies otherwise if a Will gift goes to multiple recipients if any do not survive me the part to them lapses and instead goes to other surviving recipients.
    No earlier transfer reduces a Will gift unless I usually called it a loan or advancement.
    In this Will any gender or gendered word includes all genders, and the singular includes the plural and vice versa, and "they" can mean a single person or many persons.
    Unless a Will specifically says otherwise a secured debt including a mortgage or lien shall not be paid off including by a Personal Representative or in probate, and a recipient of a Will gift of property takes it subject to debts. Also, no recipient of property who may lose it or who pays to keep it may have my estate or others pay or do exoneration.
    If at my death I somehow no longer own, possess, or otherwise control an item in a specific gift then the gift is extinguished, including I want full ademption to apply.
    I request and authorize any informal, summary, and quick probate or similar action. Any Personal Representative may act independently with no supervision of any court, including independent administration, and with no inventory, appraisal, or other action.
    Any Guardian of any type, Conservator, Custodian, or other person managing a minor's property or money may use or invade the principal and sell property without court action.
    I give any Personal Representative the a) fullest authority, discretion, and powers allowed by state law in any jurisdiction they may act, b) power to lease, sell, mortgage, convey, or keep property including real property in a manner and time they find helpful or

proper, and c) authority to settle or pay claims or debts in time and manner they choose.

Any Personal Representative may access, manage, delete, modify, transfer, and otherwise control any digital accounts and assets I had any interest in or power over.

Any Personal Representative, Executor, Administrator, Guardian of any type like for a person or estate, Conservator, Custodian, or other fiduciary under this Will or otherwise shall qualify and serve without bond, surety, security, surety bond, or similar.

No Personal Representative or any professional entitled to fair compensation shall be paid a percentage or share of my estate, property, or money even if that is standard.

The residue includes lapsed or failed gifts, insurance paid to the estate, digital assets, inheritances owed me, and all I had power of appointment or testamentary disposition over.

If evidence does not show it likely a person survived me by 120 hours (5 days) then for this Will and my estate they shall be deemed in all ways as having died before me.

Any Personal Representative may anytime transfer money or property of a minor under age 18 to a Custodian to serve under the Pennsylvania Uniform Transfers to Minors Act or similar law anywhere, and may pick a person to be Custodian including themselves.

To the extent allowed by law any Personal Representative should follow any writings I have done disposing of tangible personal property in the manner the writings indicate.

If part of this Will is by law invalid or unenforceable other provisions remain in effect.

TESTATOR

IN WITNESS WHEREOF, I, the Testator, declare I have voluntarily signed this Will on the ____ day of _____, 20____.

_____
Testator signature

WITNESSES
(optional in Pennsylvania)

The foregoing instrument was signed by the Testator in our presence and declared by the Testator to be the Testator's Will, and we, the undersigned Witnesses, sign our names hereunto to act as witnesses at the request and in the presence of the Testator, and in the presence of each other on the _____ day of _____, 20_____.

_____   _____
Signature of Witness #1   Address of Witness #1

_____   _____
Signature of Witness #2   Address of Witness #2

CHAPTER 9
FORM 3: SELF-PROVING AFFIDAVIT

FORM CAN BE DONE TO SUPPORT A WILL

This form is optional but can be done to support a Will by helping reduce later legal work. This form is a statutory form found in state law at Pa. Stat. § 3132.1 for people to find and use if they want.

FORM SAVES LATER WORK OF SHOWING WILL WAS PROPERLY SIGNED

A Self-Proving Affidavit can help "prove" after a death a Will was properly signed by the person doing the Will. If this form isn't done then to use a Will after a death a little work is required to get testimony or other evidence from people that shows it is Testator's signature. If this form is not done there is bit more legal risk a Will is not followed later. But of people doing Wills usually <u>half skip doing a Self-Proving Affidavit</u> mostly due to the hassle of finding a notary on top of witnesses each time a Will is done or re-done, and since it usually just saves work of people who are happy to testify to get property and money using a Will. About a quarter of U.S. states have no Self-Proving Affidavit at all.

FORM IS DONE BY TESTATOR AND 2 WITNESSES SIGNING WITH A NOTARY

The person who did a Will and the 2 witnesses who saw the Will signed must sign this form while they are in front of a person who is a notary. The notary can help fill out the form and then the notary also signs and notarizes the form (by using their notary ink stamp). A notary can be found and politely asked to help at banks, insurance agents, libraries, mail-copy centers, and other places. A notary also can be found by using the phonebook. The Self-Proving Affidavit form is often done minutes after a Will is signed but it also can be done much later whenever Testator and witnesses can all meet a notary. This form can't be done before a Will is done. After being done the form is often paperclipped to the Will it supports.

SELF-PROVING AFFIDAVIT
Acknowledgment

Commonwealth of Pennsylvania

County of _____

  I, _____, the Testator whose name is signed to the attached or foregoing instrument, having been duly qualified according to law, do hereby acknowledge that I signed and executed the instrument as my Will; and that I signed it willingly and as my free and voluntary act for the purposes therein expressed.

  Sworn to or affirmed and acknowledged before me by _____, the Testator, this ____ day of _____, 20___.

_____
(Testator)

_____
(Signature of officer or notary)
(Seal and official capacity of officer)

Affidavit

Commonwealth of Pennsylvania

County of _____

  We (or I), _____ and _____, the Witness(es) whose name(s) are (is) signed to the attached or foregoing instrument, being duly qualified according to law, do depose and say that we were (I was) present and saw the Testator sign and execute the instrument as Testator's Will; that the Testator signed willingly and executed it as Testator's free and voluntary act for the purposes therein expressed; that each subscribing Witness in the hearing and sight of the Testator signed the Will acting as a witness; and that to the best of our (my) knowledge the Testator was at that time 18 or more years of age, of sound mind, and under no constraint or undue influence.

  Sworn to or affirmed and subscribed to before me by _____ and _____, witness(es), this ____ day of _____, 20____.

_____   _____
Witness   Witness

_____
(Signature of officer or notary)
(Seal and official capacity of officer)

CHAPTER 10
FORM 4: DURABLE HEALTH CARE POWER OF ATTORNEY AND HEALTH CARE TREATMENT OPTIONS (LIVING WILL)

FORM CAN NAME HEALTH CARE AGENT AND GIVE INSTRUCTIONS

This form lets a person name someone to if needed control health care, give health care instructions of many kinds, and do organ donation. Note, usually paramedics and other people in a hurry won't read and follow this long form and will just give full care. This form is a statutory form found in state law at 20 Pa. Statutes § 5471, but some health care facilities use different forms for this.

IN FORM AGENT CAN BE NAMED IN POWER OF ATTORNEY PART

This form lets a person name someone as "Agent" to control their health care if needed (like if a person is later incapacitated by unconsciousness or serious mental confusion). Naming a spouse, family member, or friend here can help them not have to see a judge in a medical emergency. The part of the form naming someone as Agent is often called the "Health Care Power Of Attorney" part.

IN FORM WHEN TO STOP CARE CAN BE COVERED IN LIVING WILL PART

In the form a person can say how to stop most health care if later doctors think an incapacitated person is seriously ill and more health care is unlikely to help. This is often called the "Living Will" part of the form. Doing this is serious and hard to fill out and usually only the most sick or most elderly people do this part, and most people just skip doing any part of the Living Will area.

IN FORM GENERAL INSTRUCTIONS CAN BE COVERED

In the form a person can write general health care instructions that family, Agent, and doctors must legally follow. But many people skip instructions since they are hard to write to cover all situations, they can cause legal problems if not clear, and people trust their Agent or family to be wise and decide what to do.

IN FORM ORGAN DONATION CAN BE COVERED

In the form a person can cover what organ donation they want. But it is usually better to do this as part of drivers license or state ID paperwork, and the form's part about organ donation is often skipped.

PERSON SIGNS FORM WITH 2 WITNESSES AND MAYBE A NOTARY

To complete the form a person initials or writes in many different parts of the form. There are a few places to sign in middle of the form. Then at end of the form is a place for a person to sign in the presence of 2 persons acting as witnesses who then sign too. Anyone at least age 18 can be a witness except the person given power in the form as Health Care Agent. Many people also try not to use as witnesses any person financially tied to them, involved in giving health care to them, or any close family members.
The form at the end also gives the option to sign while with a person who is a notary, and this is not legally required but may help the form may be used in a different state. Once the form is done many people Quickly show it to places that might give care to make it part of the person's medical file to be followed.
To cancel the form a person usually says the form is cancelled to all places that saw the form.

DURABLE HEALTH CARE POWER OF ATTORNEY
AND
HEALTH CARE TREATMENT INSTRUCTIONS
(LIVING WILL)

(20 PENNSYLVANIA STATUTES § 5471)

PART I
INTRODUCTORY REMARKS ON
HEALTH CARE DECISION MAKING

You have the right to decide the type of health care you want.

Should you become unable to understand, make or communicate decisions about medical care, your wishes for medical treatment are most likely to be followed if you express those wishes in advance by:

(1) naming a health care agent to decide treatment for you; and
(2) giving health care treatment instructions to your health care agent or health care provider.

An advance health care directive is a written set of instructions expressing your wishes for medical treatment.

NOTICE ABOUT ANATOMICAL DONATION

This document may also contain directions regarding whether you wish to donate an organ, tissue or eyes. Under Pennsylvania law, donating a part of the body for transplantation or research is a voluntary act. You do not have to donate an organ, tissue, eye or other part of the body. However, it is important that you make your wishes about anatomical donation known, just as it is important to make your choices about end-of-life care known.

Surgeons have made great strides in the field of organ donation and can now transplant hands, facial tissue and limbs. A hand, facial tissue and a limb are examples of what is known as a vascularized composite allograft. Under Pennsylvania law, explicit and specific consent to donate hands, facial tissue, limbs or other vascularized composite allografts must be given. You may use this document to make clear your wish to donate or not to donate hands, facial tissue or limbs.

Under Pennsylvania law, the organ donor designation on the driver's license authorizes the individual to donate what we traditionally think of as organs (heart, lung, liver, kidney) and tissue and does not authorize the individual to donate hands, facial tissue, limbs or other vascularized composite allografts.

Detailed information about anatomical donation, including the procedure used to recover organs, tissues and eyes, can be found on the Department of Transportation's Internet website. Information about the donation of hands, facial tissue and limbs can also be found on the Department of Transportation's Internet website.

You may wish to consult with your physician or your attorney to determine whether the procedure for making an anatomical donation is compatible with fulfilling your specific choices

for end-of-life care. In addition, you may want to consult with clergy regarding whether you want to donate an organ, a hand, facial tissue or limb or other part of the body. It is important to understand that donating a hand, limb or facial tissue may have an impact on funeral arrangements and that an open casket may not be possible.

An advance health care directive may contain a health care power of attorney, where you name a person called a "health care agent" to decide treatment for you, and a living will, where you tell your health care agent and health care providers your choices regarding the initiation, continuation, withholding or withdrawal of life-sustaining treatment and other specific directions regarding end-of-life care and your views regarding organ and tissue donation.

You may limit your health care agent's involvement in deciding your medical treatment so that your health care agent will speak for you only when you are unable to speak for yourself or you may give your health care agent the power to speak for you immediately. This combined form gives your health care agent the power to speak for you only when you are unable to speak for yourself. A living will cannot be followed unless your attending physician determines that you lack the ability to understand, make or communicate health care decisions for yourself and you are either permanently unconscious or you have an end-stage medical condition, which is a condition that will result in death despite the introduction or continuation of medical treatment. You, and not your health care agent, remain responsible for the cost of your medical care.

If you do not write down your wishes about your health care in advance, and if later you become unable to understand, make or communicate these decisions, those wishes may not be honored because they may remain unknown to others.

A health care provider who refuses to honor your wishes about health care must tell you of its refusal and help to transfer you to a health care provider who will honor your wishes.

You should give a copy of your advance health care directive (a living will, health care power of attorney or a document containing both) to your health care agent, your physicians, family members and others whom you expect would likely attend to your needs if you become unable to understand, make or communicate decisions about medical care. If your health care wishes change, tell your physician and write a new advance health care directive to replace your old one. If your wishes about donating an organ, tissue or eyes change, tell your physician and write a new advance health care directive to replace your old one. If you do not wish to donate a hand, facial tissue or limb, it is important to make that clear in your advance health care directive or health care power of attorney, or both. It is important in selecting a health care agent that you choose a person you trust who is likely to be available in a medical situation where you cannot make decisions for yourself. You should inform that person that you have appointed him or her as your health care agent and discuss your beliefs and values with him or her so that your health care agent will understand your health care objectives, including whether you want to limit or withhold life-sustaining measures in the event that you become permanently unconscious or have an end-stage medical condition. You should also tell your health care agent whether you want to donate organs, tissue, eyes or other parts of the body and whether you want to make a donation of your hands, facial tissue or limbs. It is important to understand that if you decide to donate a hand, limb or facial tissue it may impact funeral arrangements and that an open casket may not be possible.

You may wish to consult with knowledgeable, trusted individuals such as family members, your physician or clergy when considering an expression of your values and health care wishes. You are free to create your own advance health care directive to convey your wishes regarding medical treatment. The following form is an example of an advance health care directive that combines a health care power of attorney with a living will.

NOTES ABOUT THE USE OF THIS FORM

If you decide to use this form or create your own advance health care directive, you should consult with your physician and your attorney to make sure that your wishes are clearly expressed and comply with the law.

If you decide to use this form but disagree with any of its statements, you may cross out those statements.

You may add comments to this form or use your own form to help your physician or health care agent decide your medical care.

This form is designed to give your health care agent broad powers to make health care decisions for you whenever you cannot make them for yourself. It is also designed to express a desire to limit or authorize care if you have an end-stage medical condition or are permanently unconscious. If you do not desire to give your health care agent broad powers, or you do not wish to limit your care if you have an end-stage medical condition or are permanently unconscious, you may wish to use a different form or create your own. YOU SHOULD ALSO USE A DIFFERENT FORM IF YOU WISH TO EXPRESS YOUR PREFERENCES IN MORE DETAIL THAN THIS FORM ALLOWS OR IF YOU WISH FOR YOUR HEALTH CARE AGENT TO BE ABLE TO SPEAK FOR YOU IMMEDIATELY. In these situations, it is particularly important that you consult with your attorney and physician to make sure that your wishes are clearly expressed, including whether you want to limit or withhold life-sustaining measures in the event that you become permanently unconscious or have an end-stage medical condition and whether you wish to donate a part of the body for transplantation or research. You should also clearly express whether or not you wish to donate hands, facial tissue or limbs.

This form allows you to tell your health care agent your goals if you have an end-stage medical condition or other extreme and irreversible medical condition, such as advanced Alzheimer's disease. Do you want medical care applied aggressively in these situations or would you consider such aggressive medical care burdensome and undesirable?

You may choose whether you want your health care agent to be bound by your instructions or whether you want your health care agent to be able to decide at the time what course of treatment the health care agent thinks most fully reflects your wishes and values.

If you are a woman and diagnosed as being pregnant at the time a health care decision would otherwise be made pursuant to this form, the laws of this Commonwealth prohibit implementation of that decision if it directs that life-sustaining treatment, including nutrition and hydration, be withheld or withdrawn from you, unless your attending physician and an obstetrician who have examined you certify in your medical record that the life-sustaining treatment:

(1) will not maintain you in such a way as to permit the continuing development and live birth of the unborn child;

(2) will be physically harmful to you; or

(3) will cause pain to you that cannot be alleviated by medication.

A physician is not required to perform a pregnancy test on you unless the physician has reason to believe that you may be pregnant.

Pennsylvania law protects your health care agent and health care providers from any legal liability for following in good faith your wishes as expressed in the form or by your health care agent's direction. It does not otherwise change professional standards or excuse negligence in the way your wishes are carried out. If you have any questions about the law, consult an attorney for guidance.

This form and explanation is not intended to take the place of specific legal or medical advice for which you should rely upon your own attorney and physician.

PART II
DURABLE HEALTH CARE POWER OF ATTORNEY

I, _____, of _____ County, Pennsylvania, appoint the person named below to be my health care agent to make health and personal care decisions for me.

Effective immediately and continuously until my death or revocation by a writing signed by me or someone authorized to make health care treatment decisions for me, I authorize all health care providers or other covered entities to disclose to my health care agent, upon my agent's request, any information, oral or written, regarding my physical or mental health, including, but not limited to, medical and hospital records and what is otherwise private, privileged, protected or personal health information, such as health information as defined and described in the Health Insurance Portability and Accountability Act of 1996 (Public Law 104-191, 110 Stat. 1936), the regulations promulgated thereunder and any other State or local laws and rules. Information disclosed by a health care provider or other covered entity may be redisclosed and may no longer be subject to the privacy rules provided by 45 C.F.R. Pt. 164.

The remainder of this document will take effect when and only when I lack the ability to understand, make or communicate a choice regarding a health or personal care decision as verified by my attending physician. My health care agent may not delegate the authority to make decisions.

MY HEALTH CARE AGENT HAS ALL OF THE FOLLOWING POWERS SUBJECT TO THE HEALTH CARE TREATMENT INSTRUCTIONS THAT FOLLOW IN PART III (CROSS OUT ANY POWERS YOU DO NOT WANT TO GIVE YOUR HEALTH CARE AGENT):

1. To authorize, withhold or withdraw medical care and surgical procedures.
2. To authorize, withhold or withdraw nutrition (food) or hydration (water) medically supplied by tube through my nose, stomach, intestines, arteries or veins.
3. To authorize my admission to or discharge from a medical, nursing, residential or similar facility and to make agreements for my care and health insurance for my care, including hospice and/or palliative care.
4. To hire and fire medical, social service and other support personnel responsible for my care.
5. To take any legal action necessary to do what I have directed.
6. To request that a physician responsible for my care issue a do-not-resuscitate (DNR) order, including an out-of-hospital DNR order, and sign any required documents and consents.
7. To authorize or refuse to authorize donation of what we traditionally think of as organs (for example, heart, lung, liver, kidney), tissue, eyes or other parts of the body.
8. To authorize or refuse to authorize donation of hands, facial tissue, limbs or other vascularized composite allografts.

APPOINTMENT OF HEALTH CARE AGENT

I appoint the following health care agent:

Health Care Agent: _____
(Name and relationship)

Address:_____

Telephone Number: Home _____ Work _____

E-mail:_____

IF YOU DO NOT NAME A HEALTH CARE AGENT, HEALTH CARE PROVIDERS WILL ASK YOUR FAMILY OR AN ADULT WHO KNOWS YOUR PREFERENCES AND VALUES FOR HELP IN DETERMINING YOUR WISHES FOR TREATMENT. NOTE THAT YOU MAY NOT APPOINT YOUR DOCTOR OR OTHER HEALTH CARE PROVIDER AS YOUR HEALTH CARE AGENT UNLESS RELATED TO YOU BY BLOOD, MARRIAGE OR ADOPTION.

APPOINTMENT OF ALTERNATIVE HEALTH CARE AGENT

If my health care agent is not readily available or if my health care agent is my spouse and an action for divorce is filed by either of us after the date of this document, I appoint the person or persons named below in the order named. (It is helpful, but not required, to name alternative health care agents.)

First Alternative Health Care Agent: _____
(Name and relationship)

Address: _____

Telephone Number: Home _____ Work _____

E-mail: _____

GUIDANCE FOR HEALTH CARE AGENT (OPTIONAL) GOALS

If I have an end-stage medical condition or other extreme irreversible medical condition, my goals in making medical decisions are as follows (insert your personal priorities such as comfort, care, preservation of mental function, etc.): _____

_____
_____
_____
_____
_____
_____
_____
_____

SEVERE BRAIN DAMAGE OR BRAIN DISEASE

If I should suffer from severe and irreversible brain damage or brain disease with no realistic hope of significant recovery, I would consider such a condition intolerable and the application of aggressive medical care to be burdensome. I therefore request that my health care agent respond to any intervening (other and separate) life-threatening conditions in the same manner as directed for an end-stage medical condition or state of permanent unconsciousness as I have indicated below.

Initials _____ I agree

Initials _____ I disagree

PART III
HEALTH CARE TREATMENT INSTRUCTIONS IN THE EVENT OF END-STAGE MEDICAL CONDITION OR PERMANENT UNCONSCIOUSNESS
(LIVING WILL)

The following health care treatment instructions exercise my right to make my own health care decisions. These instructions are intended to provide clear and convincing evidence of my wishes to be followed when I lack the capacity to understand, make or communicate my treatment decisions:

IF I HAVE AN END-STAGE MEDICAL CONDITION (WHICH WILL RESULT IN MY DEATH, DESPITE THE INTRODUCTION OR CONTINUATION OF MEDICAL TREATMENT) OR AM PERMANENTLY UNCONSCIOUS SUCH AS AN IRREVERSIBLE COMA OR AN IRREVERSIBLE VEGETATIVE STATE AND THERE IS NO REALISTIC HOPE OF SIGNIFICANT RECOVERY, ALL OF THE FOLLOWING APPLY (CROSS OUT ANY TREATMENT INSTRUCTIONS WITH WHICH YOU DO NOT AGREE):

1. I direct that I be given health care treatment to relieve pain or provide comfort even if such treatment might shorten my life, suppress my appetite or my breathing, or be habit forming.

2. I direct that all life prolonging procedures be withheld or withdrawn. You may want to consult with your physician and attorney in order to determine whether your designated choices regarding end-of-life care are compatible with anatomical donation. In order to donate an organ your body may need to be maintained on artificial support after you have been declared dead to facilitate anatomical donation. Detailed information about the procedure for being declared brain dead or dead by lack of cardiac function and information about organ donation can be found on the Department of Transportation's publicly accessible Internet website.

3. **I specifically do not want any of the following as life prolonging procedures**: (If you wish to receive any of these treatments, write "I do want" after the treatment)

heart-lung resuscitation (CPR) _____
mechanical ventilator (breathing machine) _____
dialysis (kidney machine) _____
surgery _____
chemotherapy _____
radiation treatment _____
antibiotics _____

Please indicate whether you want nutrition (food) or hydration (water) medically supplied by a tube into your nose, stomach, intestine, arteries, or veins if you have an end-stage medical condition or are permanently unconscious and there is no realistic hope of significant recovery. (Initial only one statement.)

TUBE FEEDINGS
_____ I want tube feedings to be given
OR
NO TUBE FEEDINGS
_____ I do not want tube feedings to be given.

4. If I have authorized donation of an organ (such as a heart, liver or lung) or a vascularized composite allograft in the next section of this document, I authorize the use of artificial support, including a ventilator, for a limited period of time after I am declared dead to facilitate donation.

5. I specifically **do not want to be on artificial support after I am declared dead** (Initial statement if wanted). _____

HEALTH CARE AGENT'S USE OF INSTRUCTIONS
(INITIAL ONE OPTION ONLY).

_____ My health care agent must follow these instructions.

OR

_____ These instructions are only guidance.
My health care agent shall have final say and may override any of my instructions. (Indicate any exceptions) _____

_____
_____
_____
_____
_____
_____
_____
_____
_____
_____
_____
_____
_____

If I did not appoint a health care agent, these instructions shall be followed.

LEGAL PROTECTION

Pennsylvania law protects my health care agent and health care providers from any legal liability for their good faith actions in following my wishes as expressed in this form or in complying with my health care agent's direction. **On behalf of myself, my executors and heirs, I further hold my health care agent and my health care providers harmless and indemnify them against any claim for their good faith actions in recognizing my health care agent's authority or in following my treatment instructions.**

SIGNATURE _____

INFORMATION ABOUT ANATOMICAL DONATION (OPTIONAL)

Donating an organ or other part of the body is a voluntary act. Under Pennsylvania law, you do not have to donate an organ or any other part of your body. It is important to know the effect of organ donation on your decisions about end-of-life care so that your wishes about end-of-life care will be fulfilled. If someone wishes to become an organ donor, the person may be kept on artificial support after the person has been declared dead to facilitate anatomical donation. Detailed information about the procedure for recovering organs and other parts of the body and detailed information about brain death and cardiac death may be found on the Department of Transportation's publicly accessible Internet website.

Under Pennsylvania law, the organ donor designation on the driver's license authorizes the individual to donate what we traditionally think of as organs (for example, heart, lung, liver, kidney) and tissue and does not authorize the individual to donate hands, facial tissue, limbs or other vascularized composite allografts.

Under Pennsylvania law, explicit and specific consent to donate hands, facial tissue, limbs and other vascularized composite allografts is needed. Donation of these parts of the body is voluntary. Information about the procedure to transplant hands, facial tissue and limbs can be found on the Department of Transportation's publicly accessible Internet website. It is important to know that donating a hand, limb or facial tissue may impact funeral arrangements and that an open casket may not be possible.

ORGAN DONATION

_____ (Initial statement if wanted). I **do consent** to making an anatomical gift. This gift does not include hands, facial tissue, limbs or other vascularized composite allografts. I understand that if I want to donate a hand, facial tissue, limb or other vascularized composite allograft, there is another place in this document for me to do so. I also understand the hospital may provide artificial support, which may include a ventilator, after I am declared dead in order to facilitate donation. I consent to making a gift of the following parts of my body for transplantation or research (please insert any limitations you desire on donation of specific organs or tissues or eyes or any limitation on the use of a donated part of the body): __

_____

_____

SIGNATURE _____ DATE _____

GIFT OF HANDS, FACIAL TISSUE, LIMBS AND OTHER VASCULARIZED COMPOSITE ALLOGRAFTS

_____ (Initial statement if wanted). I **do consent** to making a gift of my hands, facial tissue, limbs or other vascularized composite allografts. I also understand that I have the option of requesting reconstruction of my body in preparation for burial and that anonymity of identity may not be able to be protected in the case of donation of hands, facial tissue or limbs. I also understand that burial arrangements may be affected and that an open casket may not be possible. I also understand that the hospital may provide artificial support, which may include a ventilator, after I am declared dead in order to facilitate donation.

Please insert any limitations you desire on donation of hands, facial tissue, limbs or other vascularized composite allografts and whether you request reconstructive surgery before burial:

_____

_____

SIGNATURE _____ DATE _____

_____ (Initial statement if wanted). I **do not consent** to donating my organs, tissues or any other part of my body, including hands, facial tissue, limbs or other vascularized composite allografts. This provision serves as a refusal to donate any part of my body. This provision also serves as a revocation of any prior decision I have made to donate organs, tissues or other parts of my body, including hands, facial tissue, limbs or other vascularized composite allograft made in a prior document, including a driver's license, will, power of attorney, health care power of attorney or other document.

SIGNATURE _____ DATE _____

SIGNATURE AND COMPLETION OF THIS DOCUMENT

Having carefully read this document, I have signed it this ____ day of _____, 20_____, revoking all previous health care powers of attorney and health care treatment instructions.

SIGNATURE _____
(SIGN FULL NAME HERE FOR HEALTH CARE POWER OF ATTORNEY AND HEALTH CARE TREATMENT INSTRUCTIONS)

WITNESS:_____

WITNESS:_____

Two witnesses at least 18 years of age are required by Pennsylvania law and should witness your signature in each other's presence. A person who signs this document on behalf of and at the direction of a principal may not be a witness. (It is preferable if the witnesses are not your heirs, nor your creditors, nor employed by any of your health care providers.)

NOTARIZATION (OPTIONAL)

(Notarization of document is not required by Pennsylvania law, but if the document is both witnessed and notarized, it is more likely to be honored by the laws of some other states.)

On this _____ day of _____, 20_____, before me personally appeared the aforesaid declarant and principal, to me known to be the person described in and who executed the foregoing instrument and acknowledged that he/she executed the same as his/her free act and deed.

IN WITNESS WHEREOF, I have hereunto set my hand and affixed my official seal in the County of _____, State of _____ the day and year first above written.

_____   _____
Notary Public   My commission expires

CHAPTER 11
FORM 5: DO NOT RESUSCITATE

IN FORM CAN IMMEDIATELY REFUSE HEALTH CARE

This chapter actually has 2 forms which are similar and do the serious act of saying to immediately no longer give certain health care. Doing this is serious and usually only the sickest or oldest people do it. Both forms are often called by people the "Do Not Resuscitate" form. These are both official state forms. Both these forms are short and usually will be quickly read and followed by paramedics or similar personnel. The 2 forms are covered in the same chapter since they are similar and usually people don't do both forms. Note, even after doing a form a person is usually free to verbally override it, like by not showing the form or saying to a paramedic or doctor to give all care. Pain relief and comfort care is still given if ever needed, so if needed paramedics are still usually called to get a person this limited care.

FIRST FORM SAYS TO IMMEDIATELY NOT GIVE MANY KINDS OF CARE

This chapter's first form, the Pennsylvania Orders For Life-Sustaining Treatment form (the "P.O.L.S.T."), says to immediately no longer give the many kinds of health care listed in the form. This form often says to immediately no longer give antibiotics, artificial feeding, and C.P.R. This form is short so it can be read fast and be followed by those in a hurry like paramedics outside a health facility, but the P.O.L.S.T. form is also often used by people who are inside a care facility. Note, in recent years the P.O.L.S.T. form is used more than the older Out-Of-Hospital Do-Not-Resuscitate form.

SECOND FORM SAYS TO IMMEDIATELY NO LONGER GIVE RESUSCITATION

This chapter's second form, the Out-Of-Hospital Do-Not-Resuscitate form, says to immediately not give any resuscitation, which is trying to restart or help the hear or breathing. The term "resuscitation" covers cardio-pulmonary resuscitation (C.P.R.), defibrillation (electric shocks), and machine or tube breathing. The form is short and can be read fast and followed by paramedics and similar personnel, and generally this Out-of-Hospital Do-Not-Resuscitate form tends to be used by people outside any care facility. Some people also use a "DNR bracelet" that doctors can help people get (see photo).

FORM IS SIGNED BY DOCTOR AND A PATIENT

To be valid these forms must be signed by a person's doctor (physician) or similar health professional, and by the person doing the form (or their named representative who is authorized to do this). Usually a person's doctor provides copies of this form on nice colored paper for people to fill out. Once it is done usually people then show the form to places that may give care to then be followed. Usually a person also keeps a copy near their body to show to paramedics or similar personnel who may try to give health care.

SEND FORM WITH PERSON WHENEVER TRANSFERRED OR DISCHARGED
To follow these orders, an EMS provider must have an order from his/her medical command physician

Pennsylvania Orders for Life-Sustaining Treatment (POLST)

pennsylvania DEPARTMENT OF HEALTH

Last Name: _____
First/Middle Initial: _____
Date of Birth: _____

FIRST follow these orders, **THEN** contact physician, certified registered nurse practitioner or physician assistant. This is an Order Sheet based on the person's medical condition and wishes at the time the orders were issued. Everyone shall be treated with dignity and respect.

A — Check One
CARDIOPULMONARY RESUSCITATION (CPR): Person has no pulse and is not breathing.

☐ CPR/Attempt Resuscitation ☐ DNR/Do Not Attempt Resuscitation (Allow Natural Death)

When not in cardiopulmonary arrest, follow orders in **B**, **C** and **D**.

B — Check One
MEDICAL INTERVENTIONS: Person has pulse and/or is breathing.

☐ **COMFORT MEASURES ONLY** Use medication by any route, positioning, wound care and other measures to relieve pain and suffering. Use oxygen, oral suction and manual treatment of airway obstruction as needed for comfort. *Do not transfer* to hospital for life-sustaining treatment. *Transfer* if comfort needs cannot be met in current location.

☐ **LIMITED ADDITIONAL INTERVENTIONS** Includes care described above. Use medical treatment, IV fluids and cardiac monitor as indicated. Do not use intubation, advanced airway interventions, or mechanical ventilation.

Transfer to hospital if indicated. Avoid intensive care if possible.

☐ **FULL TREATMENT** Includes care described above. Use intubation, advanced airway interventions, mechanical ventilation, and cardioversion as indicated.

Transfer to hospital if indicated. Includes intensive care.

Additional Orders _____

C — Check One
ANTIBIOTICS:

☐ No antibiotics. Use other measures to relieve symptoms.
☐ Determine use or limitation of antibiotics when infection occurs, with comfort as goal
☐ Use antibiotics if life can be prolonged

Additional Orders

D — Check One
ARTIFICIALLY ADMINISTERED HYDRATION / NUTRITION:
Always offer food and liquids by mouth if feasible

☐ No hydration and artificial nutrition by tube.
☐ Trial period of artificial hydration and nutrition by tube.
☐ Long-term artificial hydration and nutrition by tube.

Additional Orders

E — Check One
SUMMARY OF GOALS, MEDICAL CONDITION AND SIGNATURES:

Discussed with
☐ Patient
☐ Parent of Minor
☐ Health Care Agent
☐ Health Care Representative
☐ Court-Appointed Guardian
☐ Other:

Patient Goals/Medical Condition:

By signing this form, I acknowledge that this request regarding resuscitative measures is consistent with the known desires of, and in the best interest of, the individual who is the subject of the form.

Physician /PA/CRNP Printed Name: _____   Physician /PA/CRNP Phone Number: _____

Physician/PA/CRNP Signature (Required): _____   Date: _____

Signature of Patient or Surrogate

Signature (required)	Name (print)	Relationship (write "self" if patient)

PaDOH version 06-28-2021

SEND FORM WITH PERSON WHENEVER TRANSFERRED OR DISCHARGED

Other Contact Information

Surrogate	Relationship	Phone Number	
Health Care Professional Preparing Form	Preparer Title	Phone Number	Date Prepared

Directions for Healthcare Professionals

Any individual for whom a Pennsylvania Order for Life-Sustaining Treatment form is completed should ideally have an advance health care directive that provides instructions for the individual's health care and appoints an agent to make medical decisions whenever the patient is unable to make or communicate a healthcare decision. If the patient wants a DNR Order issued in section "A", the physician/PA/CRNP should discuss the issuance of an Out-of-Hospital DNR order, if the individual is eligible, to assure that an EMS provider can honor his/her wishes. Contact the Pennsylvania Department of Aging for information about sample forms for advance health care directives. Contact the Pennsylvania Department of Health, Bureau of EMS, for information about Out-of-Hospital Do-Not-Resuscitate orders, bracelets and necklaces. POLST forms may be obtained online from the Pennsylvania Department of Health. www.health.pa.gov or www.papolst.org

Completing POLST

Must be completed by a health care professional based on patient preferences and medical indications or decisions by the patient or a surrogate. This document refers to the person for whom the orders are issued as the "individual" or "patient" and refers to any other person authorized to make healthcare decisions for the patient covered by this document as the "surrogate."

At the time a POLST is completed, any current advance directive, if available, must be reviewed.

Must be signed by a physician/PA/CRNP and patient/surrogate to be valid. Verbal orders are acceptable with follow-up signature by physician/PA/CRNP in accordance with facility/community policy. A person designated by the patient or surrogate may document the patient's or surrogate's agreement. Use of original form is strongly encouraged. Photocopies and Faxes of signed POLST forms should be respected where necessary

Using POLST

If a person's condition changes and time permits, the patient or surrogate must be contacted to assure that the POLST is updated as appropriate.

If any section is not completed, then the healthcare provider should follow other appropriate methods to determine treatment.

An automated external defibrillator (AED) should not be used on a person who has chosen "Do Not Attempt Resuscitation"

Oral fluids and nutrition must always be offered if medically feasible.

When comfort cannot be achieved in the current setting, the person, including someone with "comfort measures only," should be transferred to a setting able to provide comfort (e.g., treatment of a hip fracture).

A person who chooses either "comfort measures only" or "limited additional interventions" may not require transfer or referral to a facility with a higher level of care.

An IV medication to enhance comfort may be appropriate for a person who has chosen "Comfort Measures Only."

Treatment of dehydration is a measure which may prolong life. A person who desires IV fluids should indicate "Limited Additional Interventions" or "Full Treatment.

A patient with or without capacity or the surrogate who gave consent to this order or who is otherwise specifically authorized to do so, can revoke consent to any part of this order providing for the withholding or withdrawal of life-sustaining treatment, at any time, and request alternative treatment.

Review

This form should be reviewed periodically (consider at least annually) and a new form completed if necessary when:
  (1) The person is transferred from one care setting or care level to another, or
  (2) There is a substantial change in the person's health status, or
  (3) The person's treatment preferences change.

Revoking POLST

If the POLST becomes invalid or is replaced by an updated version, draw a line through sections A through E of the invalid POLST, write "VOID" in large letters across the form, and sign and date the form.

PENNSYLVANIA OUT-OF-HOSPITAL DNR 3/1/03
Patient's Name: Jane Doe
Attending Physician: John Smith, MD
(Printed)
(Signature): *John Smith MD*

PENNSYLVANIA OUT-OF-HOSPITAL DNR

Patient's Name: Jane Doe

Attending Physician:
(Printed): John Smith, MD
(Signature): *John Smith MD*
Date: March 1, 2003

 **OUT-OF-HOSPITAL DO-NOT-RESUSCITATE ORDER**

1. **Patient's Name:** _____

2A. Attending Physician Statement:

I, the undersigned, state that I am the attending physician of the patient named above. The above-named patient, or the patient's surrogate or other person by virtue of that person's legal relationship to the patient, has requested this order, and I have made a determination that this patient is eligible for an order and satisfies one of the following: (1) the patient has an end-stage medical condition; (2) the patient is in a terminal condition; (3) the patient is permanently unconscious and has a living will directing that no cardiopulmonary resuscitation be provided to the patient in the event of the patient's cardiac or respiratory arrest; or (4) the patient is permanently unconscious and has a living will authorizing the surrogate or other person named below to request an out-of-hospital do-not-resuscitate order for the patient. <u>I direct any and all emergency medical services personnel, commencing on the date of my signature below, to withhold cardiopulmonary resuscitation, (cardiac compression, invasive airway techniques, artificial ventilation, defibrillation and other related procedures) from the patient in</u> the event of the patient's respiratory or cardiac arrest. If the patient is not yet in cardiac or respiratory arrest, I further direct such personnel to provide to the patient other medical interventions, such as intravenous fluids, oxygen or other therapies necessary to provide comfort, care or to alleviate pain, unless directed otherwise by the patient or the emergency medical services provider's authorized medical command physician.

Signature of Physician:_____Printed:_____

Date: _____   Emergency Telephone Number:_____

Bracelet issued: _____Yes _____No   Necklace issued: _____Yes _____No

2B. Attending Physician Statement for Patient Pregnant When Order Issues (in addition to above statement):

I, the undersigned, certify that an obstetrician has examined the patient named above and that the obstetrician and I have certified in the patient's medical record as required by law that life-sustaining treatment, nutrition, hydration and cardiopulmonary resuscitation will have one of the following consequences if provided to this pregnant patient: (1) they will not maintain the pregnant patient in such a way as to permit the continuing development and live birth of the unborn child; or (2) they will be physically harmful to the pregnant patient; or (3) they will cause pain to the pregnant patient which cannot be alleviated by medication.

Signature of Physician:_____Printed:_____

Date:_____

3A. Patient's Statement:

I, the undersigned, hereby direct that in the event of my cardiac and/or respiratory arrest efforts at cardiopulmonary resuscitation not be initiated and that they may be withdrawn if initiated. I understand that I may revoke these directions at any time by giving verbal instructions to the emergency medical services providers, by physical cancellation or destruction of this form or my bracelet or necklace or by simply not displaying this form or the bracelet or the necklace for my EMS caregivers.

Date_____   _____
                                   Signature of Patient
                                   (If patient qualified to sign)

3B. Surrogate's/Other Person's (by virtue of relationship to patient) Statement:

I, the undersigned, hereby certify that I am legally authorized to execute this order on the patient's behalf by virtue of having been designated as the patient's surrogate and/or by virtue of my relationship to the patient (specify relationship: _____). I hereby direct that in the event of the patient's cardiac and/or respiratory arrest, efforts at cardiopulmonary resuscitation not be initiated and be withdrawn if initiated.

Date_____   _____
                                   Signature of Surrogate/Other Person by Virtue of Relationship to Patient
                                   (If patient not qualified to sign)

CHAPTER 12
FORM 6: GENERAL DURABLE POWER OF ATTORNEY

FORM LETS POWER BE GIVEN OVER PROPERTY, MONEY, AND MORE

This form lets a person give power to someone to let them do things with the person's money, property, debt, and other things. Many people call this a "Financial Power Of Attorney". About half of the form are language required by Pennsylvania law. Some lawyers and banks use documents with different language.

FORM GIVES POWER TO LET SOMEONE HELP WITH PROPERTY AND MONEY

This form lets a person (called in the form the "Principal") give power to someone (called in the form the "Agent" or "Attorney-in-Fact") to do things involving the Principal's money and property and other things. Doing this form can let an Agent help and do chores, pay bills, move money in accounts, buy or sell items, sign contracts, take out debt, and get information from banks and others. This can help if a person is sick, busy, or away, and may avoid need for a nursing home, conservator, or guardian. The person named Agent is usually a person like a spouse, relative, or friend. A person until incapacitated can still make decisions and overrule or fire the Agent. Some people modify the form to give instructions or limit power but if anything is unclear banks or others may be worried and not follow it. The form is called "durable" since it is still effective if a person is incapacitated, and it is called "general" since powers given are broad. If an Agent signs anything it should look like, for example, "Ed Doe signing as Agent under Power of Attorney for Ann Poe".

DUE TO RISKS INCLUDING FRAUD MANY SKIP FORM OR ASK LAWYER

Be warned, doing this form can be risky and lead to loss of money and property since an Agent can do dumb or criminal actions like stealing property, wasting money, or being careless. An Agent does have a "fiduciary duty" to use due care and act in the "best interests" of a person, so they can be sued for lack of care or criminal acts, but they later might be out of money so can't undo any harm. Usually banks or others can't be blamed for obeying an Agent. Some people ask a lawyer for advice before using this form.

SIGN FORM WITH 2 WITNESSES AND A NOTARY

This form must be signed by a person in front of 2 persons acting as witnesses who then sign, and also while in front of a person who is a notary who then notarizes and signs it. The person doing the form also must sign at the bottom of the first page. A person to be a witness usually should not be the person given power in the form and, also, usually not close family. Sometime later the person who was given power in the form must sign at the very end of the form. Once the form is completed it can be kept till needed or given immediately to the person given power. To cancel the form a person usually tells the Agent and takes back copies, and also maybe tells places that saw the form that it is cancelled.

PENNSYLVANIA
GENERAL DURABLE POWER OF ATTORNEY

NOTICE FOR POWER OF ATTORNEY

THE PURPOSE OF THIS POWER OF ATTORNEY IS TO GIVE THE PERSON YOU DESIGNATE (YOUR "AGENT") BROAD POWERS TO HANDLE YOUR PROPERTY, WHICH MAY INCLUDE POWERS TO SELL OR OTHERWISE DISPOSE OF ANY REAL OR PERSONAL PROPERTY WITHOUT ADVANCE NOTICE TO YOU OR APPROVAL BY YOU.

THIS POWER OF ATTORNEY DOES NOT IMPOSE A DUTY ON YOUR AGENT TO EXERCISE GRANTED POWERS, BUT, WHEN POWERS ARE EXERCISED, YOUR AGENT MUST USE DUE CARE TO ACT FOR YOUR BENEFIT AND IN ACCORDANCE WITH THIS POWER OF ATTORNEY.

YOUR AGENT MAY EXERCISE THE POWERS GIVEN HERE THROUGHOUT YOUR LIFETIME, EVEN AFTER YOU BECOME INCAPACITATED, UNLESS YOU EXPRESSLY LIMIT THE DURATION OF THESE POWERS OR YOU REVOKE THESE POWERS OR A COURT ACTING ON YOUR BEHALF TERMINATES YOUR AGENT'S AUTHORITY.

YOUR AGENT MUST ACT IN ACCORDANCE WITH YOUR REASONABLE EXPECTATIONS TO THE EXTENT ACTUALLY KNOWN BY YOUR AGENT AND, OTHERWISE, IN YOUR BEST INTEREST, ACT IN GOOD FAITH AND ACT ONLY WITHIN THE SCOPE OF AUTHORITY GRANTED BY YOU IN THE POWER OF ATTORNEY.

THE LAW PERMITS YOU, IF YOU CHOOSE, TO GRANT BROAD AUTHORITY TO AN AGENT UNDER POWER OF ATTORNEY, INCLUDING THE ABILITY TO GIVE AWAY ALL OF YOUR PROPERTY WHILE YOU ARE ALIVE OR TO SUBSTANTIALLY CHANGE HOW YOUR PROPERTY IS DISTRIBUTED AT YOUR DEATH. BEFORE SIGNING THIS DOCUMENT, YOU SHOULD SEEK THE ADVICE OF AN ATTORNEY AT LAW TO MAKE SURE YOU UNDERSTAND IT.

A COURT CAN TAKE AWAY THE POWERS OF YOUR AGENT IF IT FINDS YOUR AGENT IS NOT ACTING PROPERLY.

THE POWERS AND DUTIES OF AN AGENT UNDER A POWER OF ATTORNEY ARE EXPLAINED MORE FULLY IN 20 PA.C.S. CH. 56.

IF THERE IS ANYTHING ABOUT THIS FORM THAT YOU DO NOT UNDERSTAND, YOU SHOULD ASK A LAWYER OF YOUR OWN CHOOSING TO EXPLAIN IT TO YOU.

I HAVE READ OR HAD EXPLAINED TO ME THIS NOTICE AND I UNDERSTAND ITS CONTENTS.

PRINCIPAL'S SIGNATURE:_____ DATE:_____

PENNSYLVANIA
GENERAL DURABLE POWER OF ATTORNEY

WARNING: THE POWERS YOU GRANT BELOW ARE EFFECTIVE EVEN IF YOU BECOME DISABLED OR INCOMPETENT. THE POWERS GRANTED BY THIS DOCUMENT ARE BROAD AND SWEEPING AND IF YOU HAVE QUESTIONS ABOUT THESE POWERS OBTAIN COMPETENT LEGAL ADVICE. YOU MAY REVOKE THIS POWER OF ATTORNEY IF YOU LATER WISH TO DO SO.

I _____ (name and address) as Principal make this power of attorney document and do hereby appoint as my Agent
_____
(name and address), and **I hereby give this Agent all the power and authority I possess or may give** and they may do any act, deed, matter, or thing as I could do if I were personally present.

Without limiting any grant of power or authority, I specifically give my Agent in this document the following power and authority:
- To engage in tangible personal property transactions.
- To engage in banking and financial transactions.
- To engage in stock, bond and other securities transactions.
- To engage in commodity and option transactions.
- To engage in real property transactions.
- To borrow money.
- To enter safe deposit boxes.
- To engage in insurance and annuity transactions.
- To engage in retirement plan transactions.
- To handle interests in estates and trusts.
- To pursue claims and litigation.
- To receive government benefits.
- To pursue tax matters.
- To make limited gifts.
- To create a trust for my benefit.
- To make additions to an existing trust for my benefit.
- To claim an elective share of the estate of my deceased spouse.
- To authorize my admission to a medical, nursing, residential or similar facility and to enter into agreements for my care.
- To renounce fiduciary positions.
- To withdraw and receive the income or corpus of a trust.

(Optional) I hereby limit or extend the power and authority given my Agent in this document, which shall control over any other provision, as follows: _____
_____
_____
_____

THIS POWER OF ATTORNEY SHALL BE CONSTRUED AS A GENERAL DURABLE POWER OF ATTORNEY AND SHALL CONTINUE TO BE EFFECTIVE EVEN IF I BECOME DISABLED, INCAPACITATED, OR INCOMPETENT.

This document does not authorize anyone to make medical and other health care decisions.

My Agent shall be entitled to reasonable compensation for services rendered.

This power of attorney is governed by the laws of Pennsylvania.

This power of attorney is effective immediately and will continue until revoked. It is not affected by uncertainty if I am alive or uncertainty if the document is revoked.

I agree any third party who receives a copy of this document may act under it.

I agree to indemnify any 3rd party for claims related to reliance on this power of attorney.

Revocation is not effective as to a third party until they learn of the revocation.

I, the Principal, am fully informed as to all the contents of this form and understand the full import of this grant of powers to my Agent.

SIGNATURE:

Signed this _____ day of _____, 20_____ .

                                                Signature:_____

NOTARY:

State of _____)
) SS.
County of _____)

On this, the _____ day of _____, 20___, before me, a Notary Public, personally appeared _____ known to me (or satisfactorily proven) to be the person whose name is subscribed to the within instrument as the Principal, and in due form of law acknowledged that they signed the within instrument for the purposes therein contained.

IN WITNESS WHEREOF, I have hereunto set my hand and notarial seal.

                                                Signed:_____

(SEAL)   My Commission Expires: _____

TWO WITNESSES:

We, the undersigned Witnesses, hereby attest that we observed the Principal make the signature above and that we then signed our names below in the presence of the Principal and in the presence of each other.

Witness Signature: _____
Witness Address: _____

Witness Signature: _____
Witness Address: _____

ACKNOWLEDGEMENT BY AGENT:

I, _____, the named Agent, have read the attached Power of Attorney and am the person identified as the Agent for the Principal. I hereby acknowledge that when I act as agent:

> I shall act in accordance with the principal's reasonable expectations to the extent actually known by me and, otherwise, in the principal's best interest, act in good faith, and act only within the scope of authority granted to me by the principal in the power of attorney.

Agent's Signature:_____ Date:_____

CHAPTER 13
FORM 7: MEDICAL CONSENT AUTHORIZATION (OVER CHILD)

FORM LETS A PARENT GIVE POWER OVER A MINOR CHILD'S HEALTH CARE

This form lets a parent give power over health care decisions for a minor child under age 18 to someone. This is often done if a parent is away for long and someone is watching a child. Note, some people may want to do a different document often called a "Power Of Attorney Over Child", to give more power including over school, discipline, and home matters to someone who is watching a child usually for many months. This form is mostly the statutory form found in state law at 11 Pa. Statutes § 2513.

FORM GIVES POWER OVER CHILD'S HEALTH CARE

This form lets a parent give power over health care of a child under 18 to someone named in the form. This form can help if a medical problem with a child arises while they are apart from a parent and medical people feel treatment needs to be authorized fast. This person given power is sometimes called the "Agent" or the "Attorney-in-Fact". Usually the person given power can be overruled or fired anytime by the parent. A person can <u>cross out some words to not give power over some treatments</u> but <u>most people skip this to give as much power as possible just in case it helps and since they trust the person they have named</u>. The form is not usually used for minor situations like babysitting, a child spending a weekend with other family, or any time a parent can be reached quickly.

PEOPLE MUST SIGN FORM WITH A NOTARY AND 2 WITNESSES

For the form to be valid a parent must sign in front of 2 witnesses who then sign and also in front of a person who is a notary who then signs and notarizes it. Witnesses can be anyone at least 18 and not being given power in the form. Some people modify the form so 2 parents can sign and if possible doing this is recommended. Later the person given power in the form should sign the form at the very end. When completed the form can be kept until needed or handed out to the person given power in the form. To cancel the form a parent usually tells the person given power it is cancelled, takes back all copies, and maybe tells other people who saw the form that the form is cancelled and no longer to be followed. Note, the form can also be modified to let a legal guardian or legal custodian (so someone not a parent) use this form, and usually they attach a copy of a court order that gave them power to it.

MEDICAL CONSENT AUTHORIZATION
(OVER CHILD)
(Act 52 of 1999 Medical Consent Act)

I _____ am the parent of the child(ren) listed below and there are no court orders now in effect that would prohibit me from conferring the power to consent upon another person.

I, _____, do hereby confer upon _____, residing at _____ the power to consent to necessary medical or mental health treatment for the following child(ren):

1) child named _____, born on _____,
residing at _____,

2) child named _____, born on _____,
residing at _____,

3) child named _____, born on _____,
residing at _____,

and on the child(ren)'s behalf do hereby state that the power to consent which I confer shall not be affected by my subsequent disability or incapacity.

The power which I confer is specifically limited to health care and mental health care decision making, and it may be exercised only by the person named above.

The person named above may consent to the following examinations and treatment for my child(ren)

(cross out all that do not apply)

        Medical

        Dental

        Surgical

        Developmental

        Mental health

        Immunizations

and may have access to any and all records, including, but not limited to, insurance records regarding any such services.

I confer the power to consent freely and knowingly in order to provide for the child(ren) and not as result of pressure, threats or payments by any person or agency.

This document shall remain in effect until it is revoked by notifying my child(ren)'s medical, mental health care and insurance providers, in writing, and the person named above that I wish to revoke it.

In witness whereof, I have signed my name to this medical consent authorization, consisting of two (2) pages on this _____ day of _____, 20____, in _____, Pennsylvania.

Parent:
Signature of Parent: _____
Printed Name or Parent: _____

Witness 1:
Witness Signature: _____
Witness No. 1 Printed Name and Address: _____
_____

Witness 2:
Witness Signature: _____
Witness No. 2 Printed Name and Address: _____
_____

Signature of adult person who is being given power:
Signature of Person: _____

CHAPTER 14
FORM 8: STATEMENT OF CONTRARY INTENT
(OVER BODILY REMAINS)

FORM CAN NAME PERSON TO CONTROL FUNERAL AND RELATED MATTERS

This form lets a person be named to later control decisions involving a dead body, burial, cremation, and related matters. This form is rarely done and usually closest family members are left in charge of this.

IN FORM CAN NAME AGENT TO CONTROL FUNERAL AND RELATED MATTERS

In the form a person can be named to be "Agent" to later make decisions about funeral, burial, cremation, cemetery, and related matters. <u>If the form is not done by law the closest family control all this</u> starting with spouse, adult children, parents of a person, and then siblings. Most people do <u>not</u> use this form, and usually only if a person thinks family may manage things badly or pick unwanted things is this form done. Payment for all these things will come from pre-paid funeral accounts, insurance, and decedent's money and property. The person given power in the form, or family if they are left in charge, should do what a person said or wrote they wanted done if the money and property in the dead person's estate can afford it. In the form are areas to write instructions but many people skip this and just talk to their Agent or family and trust them.

TO COMPLETE FORM IT JUST MUST BE SIGNED

The form to be completed just must be signed, however it is common to also have 2 people sign as witnesses and these can be anyone over age 18. The form should be kept so it can be found quickly within a day of a death or it can be given immediately to someone trusted to hold till needed.

STATEMENT OF CONTRARY INTENT (OVER BODILY REMAINS)

I, _____, hereby appoint _____ as my Agent for body disposition and other matters. My Agent shall have the sole right to determine the disposition of my body at my death and all related matters including funeral, burial, cremation, ceremonies, decorations, and similar issues. No other person regardless of his or her kinship status to me or status as my spouse shall override my Agent's authority.

If I do not give instructions below to the person I appointed they still shall have the power and authority I described above and as provided them by law.

I direct my Agent follow these instructions to the degree they can be reasonably accomplished (I understand I may leave blank any areas below):

I give the following instructions (may include about burial, cremation, coffin type, embalming, ceremonies like wake and funeral, and burial site details):

_____
_____
_____
_____
_____
_____
_____
_____
_____
_____
_____
_____

(attach additional sheets as necessary)

_____   _____
Signature   Date

Signature of Witnesses (optional)

_____   _____

APPENDIX:
HOW TO GET FORMS AND SAMPLE FILLED OUT FORMS

TO GET FORMS TO USE PEOPLE CAN:
  (1) PHOTOCOPY BOOK PAGES,
  (2) TEAR OUT PAGES FROM A BOOK, OR
  (3) DOWNLOAD BOOK WITH FORMS FROM WWW.DAVENPORTPUBLISHING.COM
AND USUALLY A PDF FORM AT IS BEST TO AVOID SPACING/FORMAT CHANGES.

EMAIL ANY COMMENTS TO DAVENPORTPRESS@GMAIL.COM.

On the next pages to show how it can be done are some filled out legal forms which are shown as samples so people can see how it is done.

People can add words to legal forms by computer or typewriter to be neater, but many people just by hand use pen, marker, or pencil to handwrite words into forms.

It is not required but is bit better if signatures are in ink or marker not pencil.

Many parts of the forms especially Will gifts can be left empty and unfilled.

Anyone can fill in words in legal form not just the person doing the form, like a friend who has neat writing can fill in all the words, addresses, and dates that are needed. Only the final signatures must be done by each person who is doing the form.

To add words in form by pen, pencil, typewriter, or computer any of these is fine:
  "I appoint ___*John Doe*___ as Agent",
  "I appoint ___John Doe___ as Agent",
  "I appoint John Doe as Agent".

When doing forms it may help to know "respectively" means "in order just stated".

People need not worry about neatness or small mistakes, and a document is usually fine if those people who knew a decedent in life can tell the likely meaning.

Sample Filled Out Form: Last Will and Testament (Standard) with Gifts section skipped to not bother making small gifts

LAST WILL AND TESTAMENT

I, _Paul Samuel Maxwell_, of _Chester County_, Pennsylvania, do revoke all prior Wills and testamentary documents and do make, publish, and declare this as my Will. I am of sound mind and under no duress or undue influence and acting voluntarily.

1. LIST OF SPOUSE AND CHILDREN. To help show I am mentally competent and have sufficient memory to make a Will I wish to list any living spouse and living children I now have. I currently have the following living spouse and living children:

none

2. GIFTS. I give these gifts in this Will, but to get a gift in this section the recipient must survive me except as otherwise stated below.

I give _____ to _____.
I give _____ to _____.
I give _____ to _____.
I give _____ to _____.
I give _____ to _____.
I give _____ to _____.
I give _____ to _____.
I give _____ to _____.

SKIPPED

3. RESIDUE. I give the rest and residue and remainder of my estate, my money and property of any kind and nature, and anything I have an interest in so long as it was not transferred by other Will provisions (all of which is called the "residue"), as follows:

a) to _Susan Lee Maxwell my sister_ who survive me with persons just named who survive me taking the share of non-survivors, then if anything remains

b) to _Oscar David Maxwell and Jennifer Judy Tabor_ and if any of those just named do not survive me their part goes to their lineal descendants, per stirpes.

4. ADMINISTRATION. I nominate and appoint _Susan Lee Maxwell_ as Personal Representative including for me, my Will, and my estate.

5. MISCELLANEOUS. The following applies to this Will and generally.

In this Will no part left unfilled is a mistake including spaces in the residue clause.

The facts support and I want Pennsylvania state law to apply to this Will and my estate.

If context allows the terms Personal Representative and Executor and Administrator are interchangeable. If context allows the terms Guardian of the Estate and Conservator and Guardian of Property and Custodian are interchangeable. Any such person has all powers and rights of the others.

I order that my just debts, funeral and related expenses, and taxes be paid as soon after my death as practical but only those items my Executor chooses to pay.

Priority of Will gifts of the same type is based on the order they are written.

The words "give" and "gift" also means a devise, bequest, grant, legacy, or similar.

I am intentionally not providing by Will or other ways for some family, including I am not providing for some children of mine and also children of a deceased child of mine.

If a gift Will reasonably mentions survival then survival is an absolute condition and anti-lapse laws or similar provisions have no effect and without survival the gift lapses. Unless a Will gift specifies otherwise if a Will gift goes to multiple recipients if any do not survive me the part to them lapses and instead goes to other surviving recipients.

No earlier transfer reduces a Will gift unless I usually called it a loan or advancement.

In this Will any gender or gendered word includes all genders, and the singular includes the plural and vice versa, and "they" can mean a single person or many persons.

Unless a Will specifically says otherwise a secured debt including a mortgage or lien shall not be paid off including by a Personal Representative or in probate, and a recipient of a Will gift of property takes it subject to debts. Also, no recipient of property who may lose it or who pays to keep it may have my estate or others pay or do exoneration.

If during my life I disposed of an item in a specific gift then the gift is extinguished, including ademption shall apply and it shall adeem.

I request and authorize any informal, summary, and quick probate or similar action. Any Personal Representative may act independently with no supervision of any court, including independent administration, and with no inventory, appraisal, or other action.

Any Guardian of any type, Conservator, Custodian, or other person managing a minor's property or money may use or invade the principal and sell property without court action.

I give any Personal Representative the a) fullest authority, discretion, and powers allowed by state law in any jurisdiction they may act, b) power to lease, sell, mortgage, convey, or keep property including real property in a manner and time they find helpful or proper, and c) authority to settle or pay claims or debts in time and manner they choose.

Any Personal Representative may access, manage, delete, modify, transfer, and otherwise control any digital accounts and assets I had any interest in or power over.

Any Personal Representative, Executor, Administrator, Guardian of any type like for a person or estate, Conservator, Custodian, or other fiduciary under this Will or otherwise

shall qualify and serve without bond, surety, security, surety bond, or similar.

No Personal Representative, lawyer, or other professional entitled to fair compensation shall be paid a percentage or share of my estate, property, or money even if it is standard.

The residue includes lapsed or failed gifts, insurance paid to the estate, digital assets, inheritances owed me, and all I had power of appointment or testamentary disposition over.

If evidence does not show it likely a person survived me by 120 hours (5 days) then for this Will and my estate they shall be deemed in all ways as having died before me.

Any Personal Representative may anytime transfer money or property of a minor under age 18 to a Custodian to serve under the Pennsylvania Uniform Transfers to Minors Act or similar law anywhere, and may pick a person to be Custodian including themselves.

To the extent allowed by law any Personal Representative should follow any writings I have done disposing of tangible personal property in the manner the writings indicate.

If part of this Will is by law invalid or unenforceable other provisions remain in effect.

TESTATOR

IN WITNESS WHEREOF, I, the Testator, declare I have voluntarily signed this Will on the _8th_ day of ___June___, 20_22_.

Paul Samuel Maxwell
Testator signature

WITNESSES
(optional in Pennsylvania)

The foregoing instrument was signed by the Testator in our presence and declared by the Testator to be the Testator's Will, and we, the undersigned Witnesses, sign our names hereunto to act as witnesses at the request and in the presence of the Testator, and in the presence of each other on the _8th_ day of ___June___, 20_22_.

Susan Ann Moon   _14 2nd St., Harrisburg, PA 18254_
Signature of Witness #1   Address of Witness #1

Eve Mable Walker   _35 Buffalo Road, Denver, Colorado 80101_
Signature of Witness #2   Address of Witness #2

Sample Filled Out Form: Last Will and Testament (Guardian)
with many gifts in Gifts section, Guardian Clause used, and Residue Given By Percentages

LAST WILL AND TESTAMENT

I, __Paul Brian Baker__, of __York County__, Pennsylvania, do revoke all prior Wills and testamentary documents and do make, publish, and declare this as my Will. I am of sound mind and under no duress or undue influence and acting voluntarily.

1. LIST OF SPOUSE AND CHILDREN. To help show I am mentally competent and have sufficient memory to make a Will I wish to list any living spouse and living children I now have. I currently have the following living spouse and living children:

__Ruth May Baker wife__   __Oscar Elliot Baker young son__
__Karen Lisa Lundy daughter__   __Derek Rupert Baker son__.

2. GIFTS. I give these gifts in this Will, but to get a gift in this section the recipient must survive me except as otherwise stated below.

I give __big oak table__ to __Anne J. Smith__.
I give __$5,000 and Ford Truck__ to __Loretta Marsha Baxter__.
I give __buildings, land, and fixtures at 63 Wentworth Road, Allentown, Pennsylvania,__ to __Kenneth Alan Ford__.
I give __all real property and fixtures I own in Bucks County in Pennsylvania__ to __Amy Marie Fox and Pamela Sue Fox__.
I give __903 Iceberg Road, Anchorage, Alaska__ to __James Eric Hanson__.
I give __Irish jewelry and my wedding ring__ to __Mary Natalie Swanson__.
I give __all jewelry not given above__ to __Kay Baxter and Mary Baxter__.
I give __$781.35__ to __Mary Natalie Swanson and Kevin Kilby__.
I give __Wells Fargo acct ending in #8923__ to __Lawrence Deer a hunting buddy__.
I give __all spare tires and auto parts__ to __Victor Perez my mechanic__.

3. RESIDUE. I give the rest and residue and remainder of my estate, my money and property of any kind and nature, and anything I have an interest in so long as it was not transferred by other Will provisions (all of which is called the "residue"), as follows:

a) to __Ruth May Baker__ who survive me with persons just named who survive me taking the share of non-survivors, then if anything remains

b) to __45% to Oscar Elliot Baker, and 45% to Karen Lisa Lundy, and 10% to Hector Sanchez my friend from the Army__ and if any of those just named do not survive me their part goes to their lineal descendants, per stirpes.

4. ADMINISTRATION. I nominate and appoint ___Ruth May Baker___
as Personal Representative including for me, my Will, and my estate.

5. GUARDIAN. I name, nominate, and appoint ___Amanda Sue Brubaker my sister___
to be Guardian of the Person of any minor child of mine and also to have care, authority, custody, and other control of them. I name, nominate, and appoint this same person to be Guardian of the Estate for any minor child and to have care, control, and power over their property, money, and estate.

6. MISCELLANEOUS. The following applies to this Will and generally.

In this Will no part left unfilled is a mistake including spaces in the residue clause.

The facts support and I want Pennsylvania state law to apply to this Will and my estate.

If context allows the terms Personal Representative and Executor and Administrator are interchangeable. If context allows the terms Guardian of the Estate and Conservator and Guardian of Property and Custodian are interchangeable. Any such person has all powers and rights of the others.

I order that my just debts, funeral and related expenses, and taxes be paid as soon after my death as practical but only those items my Executor chooses to pay.

Priority of Will gifts of the same type is based on the order they are written.

The words "give" and "gift" also means a devise, bequest, grant, legacy, or similar.

I am intentionally not providing by Will or other ways for some family, including I am not providing for some children of mine and also children of a deceased child of mine.

If a gift Will reasonably mentions survival then survival is an absolute condition and anti-lapse laws or similar provisions have no effect and without survival the gift lapses. Unless a Will gift specifies otherwise if a Will gift goes to multiple recipients if any do not survive me the part to them lapses and instead goes to other surviving recipients.

No earlier transfer reduces a Will gift unless I usually called it a loan or advancement.

In this Will any gender or gendered word includes all genders, and the singular includes the plural and vice versa, and "they" can mean a single person or many persons.

Unless a Will specifically says otherwise a secured debt including a mortgage or lien shall not be paid off including by a Personal Representative or in probate, and a recipient of a Will gift of property takes it subject to debts. Also, no recipient of property who may lose it or who pays to keep it may have my estate or others pay or do exoneration.

If during my life I disposed of an item in a specific gift then the gift is extinguished, including ademption shall apply and it shall adeem.

I request and authorize any informal, summary, and quick probate or similar action. Any Personal Representative may act independently with no supervision of any court, including independent administration, and with no inventory, appraisal, or other action.

Any Guardian of any type, Conservator, Custodian, or other person managing a minor's property or money may use or invade the principal and sell property without court action.

I give any Personal Representative the a) fullest authority, discretion, and powers allowed by state law in any jurisdiction they may act, b) power to lease, sell, mortgage,

convey, or keep property including real property in a manner and time they find helpful or proper, and c) authority to settle or pay claims or debts in time and manner they choose.

Any Personal Representative may access, manage, delete, modify, transfer, and otherwise control any digital accounts and assets I had any interest in or power over.

Any Personal Representative, Executor, Administrator, Guardian of any type like for a person or estate, Conservator, Custodian, or other fiduciary under this Will or otherwise shall qualify and serve without bond, surety, security, surety bond, or similar.

No Personal Representative, lawyer, or other professional entitled to fair compensation shall be paid a percentage or share of my estate, property, or money even if it is standard.

The residue includes lapsed or failed gifts, insurance paid to the estate, digital assets, inheritances owed me, and all I had power of appointment or testamentary disposition over.

If evidence does not show it likely a person survived me by 120 hours (5 days) then for this Will and my estate they shall be deemed in all ways as having died before me.

Any Personal Representative may anytime transfer money or property of a minor under age 18 to a Custodian to serve under the Pennsylvania Uniform Transfers to Minors Act or similar law anywhere, and may pick a person to be Custodian including themselves.

To the extent allowed by law any Personal Representative should follow any writings I have done disposing of tangible personal property in the manner the writings indicate.

If part of this Will is by law invalid or unenforceable other provisions remain in effect.

TESTATOR

IN WITNESS WHEREOF, I, the Testator, declare I have voluntarily signed this Will on the 30th day of December, 20 21.

Paul Brian Baker
Testator signature

WITNESSES
(optional in Pennsylvania)

The foregoing instrument was signed by the Testator in our presence and declared by the Testator to be the Testator's Will, and we, the undersigned Witnesses, sign our names hereunto to act as witnesses at the request and in the presence of the Testator, and in the presence of each other on the 30th day of December, 20 21.

Olivia Anna Paulson   82 Forest Road, Reading, PA 15063
Signature of Witness #1   Address of Witness #1

Matthew John Paulson   82 Forest Road, Reading, PA 15063
Signature of Witness #2   Address of Witness #2

**Sample Filled Out Form: Last Will and Testament (Standard)
with Will modified to have less gifts and to have a 1 part residue clause**

LAST WILL AND TESTAMENT

I, _John David Smith_, of _Lancaster County_, Pennsylvania, do revoke all prior Wills and testamentary documents and do make, publish, and declare this as my Will. I am of sound mind and under no duress or undue influence and acting voluntarily.

1. LIST OF SPOUSE AND CHILDREN. To help show I am mentally competent and have sufficient memory to make a Will I wish to list any living spouse and living children I now have. I currently have the following living spouse and living children:

my son Adam Michael Smith.

2. GIFTS. I give these gifts in this Will, but to get a gift in this section the recipient must survive me except as otherwise stated below.

I give _$200_ to _each of my nieces and nephews so about $2,800 in total_.

I give _$400_ to _Post Food Shelf in Pittsburgh, Pennsylvania_.

I give _$340_ to _my old church Sacred Heart in Pueblo, Colorado_.

3. RESIDUE. The rest and residue and remainder of my estate, my property of any kind and nature, and anything I have an interest in, I give to _Adam Michael Smith and Judy Paula Ford_ who survive me and to the lineal descendants per stirpes of a person just named who did not survive me.

4. ADMINISTRATION. I nominate and appoint _Judy Paula Ford my sister_ as Personal Representative including for me, my Will, and my estate.

5. MISCELLANEOUS. The following applies to this Will and generally.
  In this Will no part left unfilled is a mistake including spaces in the residue clause.
  The facts support and I want Pennsylvania state law to apply to this Will and my estate.
  If context allows the terms Personal Representative and Executor and Administrator are interchangeable. If context allows the terms Guardian of the Estate and Conservator and Guardian of Property and Custodian are interchangeable. Any such person has all powers and rights of the others.

I order that my just debts, funeral and related expenses, and taxes be paid as soon after my death as practical but only those items my Executor chooses to pay.

Priority of Will gifts of the same type is based on the order they are written.

The words "give" and "gift" also means a devise, bequest, grant, legacy, or similar.

I am intentionally not providing by Will or other ways for some family, including I am not providing for some children of mine and also children of a deceased child of mine.

If a gift Will reasonably mentions survival then survival is an absolute condition and anti-lapse laws or similar provisions have no effect and without survival the gift lapses. Unless a Will gift specifies otherwise if a Will gift goes to multiple recipients if any do not survive me the part to them lapses and instead goes to other surviving recipients.

No earlier transfer reduces a Will gift unless I usually called it a loan or advancement.

In this Will any gender or gendered word includes all genders, and the singular includes the plural and vice versa, and "they" can mean a single person or many persons.

Unless a Will specifically says otherwise a secured debt including a mortgage or lien shall not be paid off including by a Personal Representative or in probate, and a recipient of a Will gift of property takes it subject to debts. Also, no recipient of property who may lose it or who pays to keep it may have my estate or others pay or do exoneration.

If during my life I disposed of an item in a specific gift then the gift is extinguished, including ademption shall apply and it shall adeem.

I request and authorize any informal, summary, and quick probate or similar action. Any Personal Representative may act independently with no supervision of any court, including independent administration, and with no inventory, appraisal, or other action.

Any Guardian of any type, Conservator, Custodian, or other person managing a minor's property or money may use or invade the principal and sell property without court action.

I give any Personal Representative the a) fullest authority, discretion, and powers allowed by state law in any jurisdiction they may act, b) power to lease, sell, mortgage, convey, or keep property including real property in a manner and time they find helpful or proper, and c) authority to settle or pay claims or debts in time and manner they choose.

Any Personal Representative may access, manage, delete, modify, transfer, and otherwise control any digital accounts and assets I had any interest in or power over.

Any Personal Representative, Executor, Administrator, Guardian of any type like for a person or estate, Conservator, Custodian, or other fiduciary under this Will or otherwise shall qualify and serve without bond, surety, security, surety bond, or similar.

No Personal Representative, lawyer, or other professional entitled to fair compensation shall be paid a percentage or share of my estate, property, or money even if it is standard.

The residue includes lapsed or failed gifts, insurance paid to the estate, digital assets, inheritances owed me, and all I had power of appointment or testamentary disposition over.

If evidence does not show it likely a person survived me by 120 hours (5 days) then for this Will and my estate they shall be deemed in all ways as having died before me.

Any Personal Representative may anytime transfer money or property of a minor under

age 18 to a Custodian to serve under the Pennsylvania Uniform Transfers to Minors Act or similar law anywhere, and may pick a person to be Custodian including themselves.

To the extent allowed by law any Personal Representative should follow any writings I have done disposing of tangible personal property in the manner the writings indicate.

If part of this Will is by law invalid or unenforceable other provisions remain in effect.

TESTATOR

IN WITNESS WHEREOF, I, the Testator, declare I have voluntarily signed this Will on the __21st__ day of _____June_____, 20__23__.

John David Smith
Testator signature

WITNESSES
(optional in Pennsylvania)

The foregoing instrument was signed by the Testator in our presence and declared by the Testator to be the Testator's Will, and we, the undersigned Witnesses, sign our names hereunto to act as witnesses at the request and in the presence of the Testator, and in the presence of each other on the __21st__ day of _____June_____, 20__23__.

Mark Elliot Potter   2 Spruce St, Sherwood, PA 18432
Signature of Witness #1   Address of Witness #1

Ann Paula Blom   80 Oak Road, Goddard, PA 15405
Signature of Witness #2   Address of Witness #2

Sample Filled Out Form: Self-Proving Affidavit

SELF-PROVING AFFIDAVIT
Acknowledgment

Commonwealth of Pennsylvania

County of __Lancaster__

I, __John David Smith__, the Testator whose name is signed to the attached or foregoing instrument, having been duly qualified according to law, do hereby acknowledge that I signed and executed the instrument as my Will; and that I signed it willingly and as my free and voluntary act for the purposes therein expressed.

Sworn to or affirmed and acknowledged before me by __John David Smith__, the Testator, this __21st__ day of __June__, 20__23__.

John David Smith
(Testator)

NOTARIAL SEAL
Johnny C. Parker, Notary Public
City of Philadelphia, Philadelphia County
My Commission Expires June 17, 2038

Johnny C. Parker
(Signature of officer or notary)
(Seal and official capacity of officer)

Affidavit

We (or I), __Mark Elliot Potter__ and __Ann Paula Blom__, the Witness(es) whose name(s) are (is) signed to the attached or foregoing instrument, being duly qualified according to law, do depose and say that we were (I was) present and saw the Testator sign and execute the instrument as Testator's Will; that the Testator signed willingly and executed it as Testator's free and voluntary act for the purposes therein expressed; that each subscribing Witness in the hearing and sight of the Testator signed the Will acting as a witness; and that to the best of our (my) knowledge the Testator was at that time 18 or more years of age, of sound mind, and under no constraint or undue influence.

Sworn to or affirmed and subscribed to before me by __Mark Elliot Potter__ and __Ann Paula Blom__, witness(es), this __21st__ day of __June__, 20__23__.

Mark Elliot Potter
Witness

Ann Paula Blom
Witness

NOTARIAL SEAL
Johnny C. Parker, Notary Public
City of Philadelphia, Philadelphia County
My Commission Expires June 17, 2038

Johnny C. Parker
(Signature of officer or notary)
(Seal and official capacity of officer)

www.ingramcontent.com/pod-product-compliance
Lightning Source LLC
Chambersburg PA
CBHW060417220526
45465CB00008B/2918